INTERNATIONAL FOOTBALL BOOK

No. 10

Kicking up the mud and the action! – A classic clash between forward and goalkeeper. West Bromwich Albion 'keeper John Osborne, floored and desperate, scrambles the ball for a corner while Liverpool's inside-forward Alf Arrowsmith makes a late, unavailing leap . . .

INTERNATIONAL FOOTBALL BOOK

No. 10

Edited by Stratton Smith

Contributing Editors :
PETER JONES and ERIC BATTY

with contributions by

MATT BUSBY, C.B.E.   ALAN BALL

JOCK STEIN   KEN DODD   GEORGE BEST

WILLIE HENDERSON   JANOS FARKAS   JIM McCALLIOG

ANTONIO UBALDO RATTIN   BILLY BREMNER   TONY HATELEY

RON GREENWOOD   PROFESSOR JOHN COHEN   LEO HORN

BRIAN GLANVILLE   JOHAN CRUYFF   TERRY VENABLES

JOSEF MASOPUST   KURT HAMRIN   JOHN BLAIR

HELMUT HALLER   GORDON JEFFERY

SOUVENIR PRESS LTD . LONDON

*First published by Souvenir Press Ltd., London, W.1, and
simultaneously in Canada by The Ryerson Press, Toronto, 2.*

SBN.285 . 50185.2

*Printed in Great Britain by
Thomas Nelson (Printers) Ltd., London and Edinburgh.*

CONTENTS

CONTENTS—*continued*

LIST OF ILLUSTRATIONS

LIST OF ILLUSTRATIONS—*continued*

WORLD'S BEST RIGHT HERE IN BRITAIN !

by BILLY BREMNER

(Leeds United and Scotland)

'YOU are the greatest. Get out there and don't worry about what they can do. Let them worry about you.' Cassius Clay has nothing on Don Revie, our boss at Elland Road, when he is in the middle of his pep talk before we go out on to the field for an important game.

I suppose that he works on the assumption that if you tell folks a thing often enough they believe it in the end. But whatever the reasons his applied psychology seems to work and we are usually able to pull something out of the hat when the big occasion calls for it.

The best of the lot of us at that is England centre-half and Player of the Year Jackie Charlton. Big Jack has the wonderful ability to lift his game to any heights to meet the big threat. The 'big time' inspires him and no-one will ever forget his magnificent displays against some of the best centre-forwards in the world.

Uwe Seeler of West Germany, the towering Torres of Portugal and the slick Artime of Argentine all came the same to him.

West Ham's Bobby Moore was voted the 'Player of the Tournament' – but Jackie Charlton was not a cat's-whisker behind him. He tells me his personal form, and that of the whole England team in the succession of brilliant victories which put us right back on top of the world, were a direct result of the confidence and courage of England team manager Sir Alf Ramsey.

He knew exactly what he was doing when a week before the competition started he stuck his neck out and told the world's Press, 'We will win the World Cup.' It had just the effect for which he aimed.

His players, written off by many people as potential winners, lifted up their heads and walked tall and full of confidence. They let the others do the worrying.

With all due respect to Sir Alf – and the boss –

9

'Big Jack has the wonderful ability to lift his game to any heights' –
Bremner's Leeds team-mate Jackie Charlton goes up to head home a goal
against Chelsea.

there are some players you just cannot afford not to worry about. Give them an inch – they take a yard. Let your attention wander for a solitary second – and you find yourself right up the creek.

Such a gentleman is Pelé, the idol of all Brazilian Soccer fans and true lovers of the game throughout the world. When I think of him I automatically think of the juiciest black eye I ever had in my life.

It was Mr. Pelé who dished it out when I was a member of the Scottish international side which played against Brazil at Hampden in a warm-up game for the South Americans just before they took part in the World Cup.

My orders that day were to stick to him like glue. If he went off the field for attention I virtually had to stand with him on the touch-line to pick him up again the second he stepped back on to the field.

Looking back on the game I still get a certain amount of satisfaction about the way I did the job. The first chance I had I let him know I was 'on the park' with as hard a tackle for the ball as I have ever mustered.

After that, I have found most of the so-called 'greats' just do not want to know. But not Pelé.

He's not much bigger or heavier than myself, but the next time we clashed I knew all about it. We both went all-out for a high ball together and I must admit I was expecting him to draw back in the last split second. But the next thing I knew I was on the ground nursing as good a 'shiner' as you will see in many a long day.

It was entirely accidental, of course, but he

proved to me once and for all times, that he has the courage and guts which, in my book, are just as much a part of greatness as fantastic ability.

No matter how tightly I marked him I found him finding a couple of yards out of nothing. I do not think that there is a player in the world who could cut him out of a game entirely. I know I tried my level best and he still found the room to show enough of his brilliant control and balance and his two powerful feet to bring home to me that he was every bit as good as I had read.

And while I am on about 'reading', let me say that by and large I think the Press lads do a magnificent job. I should know because I have had the 'treatment' from them at both ends of the scale.

And I hope I am not going to offend anyone when I say that sometimes they seem to do their level best to frighten British players to death with the superlatives they use to describe the men they are due to play against in teams from abroad.

Men like Portugal's Eusebio, West Germany's Helmut Haller and Rivera of Italy are undoubtedly great players in their own right. But they are not the supermen they would have us believe. Take my word for it, for I have played against nearly all of them for either Scotland or Leeds United in European competition.

Eusebio, probably the pick of them, is a magnificent specimen of an athlete with a load of talent.

11

'He moves so sweetly with the ball I could watch him all day' – thus Bremner on Bobby Charlton, seen here in England colours, coming away from Scotland's Jim McCalliog, and Bremner himself.

Physically strong, he loves to go forward at great pace and have a crack at the goal in the fashion of Manchester United's inimitable George Best.

But he has yet to learn when to part with the ball and does not want to know about the defensive side of a midfield man's game. And believe me, that is of prime importance these days.

It is my considered opinion that, with the exception of Pelé, there is scarcely a 'foreigner' who could stand up to the fierce competition of a full season in the English First Division. And that is not taking into account F.A. Cup, League Cup and all the other commitments.

There is not the slightest doubt in my mind that British football, now the full value of tactical play has really sunk home, is consistently producing the best players in the world.

As a half-back I am mainly concerned with the men I have to face, and in what other country can you find such men as Ireland's George Best, Scotland's Denis Law, and Jimmy Greaves and Geoff Hurst of England. It is enough to give a defender nightmares.

The one man I would put in the same street with Pelé is Manchester United's Bobby Charlton.

He moves so sweetly with the ball I could watch him all day. His change of pace and direction are phenomenal and there are goalkeepers galore in this country and abroad who can vouch for the terrific power and accuracy he has in either foot.

When Bobby figures on the team sheet of our opponents the boss does not come any of the patter about 'not worrying about the others'. His instructions are sharp and right to the point: 'Cut out Bobby and we are halfway there.' And that is as big a tribute as Don Revie and Leeds United can pay to anyone.

No, fiery Billy Bremner is not here 'feeling the arm of the Law', in the person of referee Ray Tinkler – he's simply protesting about a foul by Sunderland forwards against grounded Leeds and Wales' 'keeper Gary Sprake. THIS PAGE, RIGHT, another sort of Law – Manchester United's Denis, completing an overhead kick for Scotland, with England's George Cohen right way up . . . but as mystified as if he, too, was standing on his head.

ALAN BALL

Better small after all . . . ?

by ALAN BALL
(Everton and England)

AR be it for me to start arguing the academic issues with schoolmasters. I accept that they are likely to leave me stranded. But when I heard the verdict of one, not so long ago, concerning the chances of a certain lad making the grade as a professional footballer I jumped in with both feet.

The doubt being expressed concerned not the boy's ability for his age, but his size. This lack of physical stature, it was suggested, could well be the reason for his not becoming a top-class footballer in the First Division. My immediate reaction was to answer: 'Rubbish!'

I should know what I'm talking about, on this particular subject. I remember all too well how, after twenty minutes of a trial for Lancashire Schoolboys, I was hauled off the field and heard the verdict: 'He's too small.'

It was a bitter moment for me – I could have wept enough tears to flood that football pitch. But maybe that harsh-sounding verdict had something to do with the fact that I *did* make the grade. Maybe it helped, even if I wasn't conscious of the fact, to make me determined to prove that I was

good enough, even if I lacked the inches.

When I was 16, and that's not so long ago, I had put all thoughts of schooling behind me, having failed my G.C.E. in all the seven subjects I had taken. Instead, I pleaded with my Dad to let me become a professional footballer.

We had a real family conference after the exam. results came out. It finished with me making an extremely bold forecast. I said simply: 'If you let me play football for a living, I promise you that I'll be playing for England by the time I'm 20.' I kept that vow, with some months to spare.

I'm not suggesting for one moment that it was all plain sailing. I was lucky in having a father who knew what the game of Soccer was all about. My Dad is a qualified F.A. coach, and he was able to help me a great deal.

But it didn't stop there. Blackpool were bold, too, in that they gave me the chance to go into top-class football. If they had taken the view that I wasn't big enough, the name of Alan Ball might never have appeared on an England team sheet.

However, the whole thing boils down to this – that Alan Ball, who stands 5 foot 6¾ inches tall and weighs 10 stone,

'My England buddy Nobby Stiles of Manchester United . . . he's tigerish in the tackle and he reads a game tremendously well' – Stiles, left, has a shot charged down by Aston Villa 'keeper Colin Withers, after beating off a tackle from John Sleeuwenhoek.

is the living proof that you don't have to be a giant wearing canal barges for football boots to make your way in the game.

There's long been a saying in Soccer that 'If you're good enough, you're old enough.' The same applies where size is concerned. Just go through the list of players who have found fame in big-time football. As a matter of fact, I've been doing some homework on the subject. . . .

Let's start at around 5 foot 8 inches – at the top, as you might say. Here are two examples it would be hard to better. First, England's World Cup left-back Ray Wilson – a team-mate of mine at Everton, and a player whose speed and skill have placed him among the world's best players. The second man? – Tottenham's Dave Mackay. . . .

Here is a wing-half famed and feared for his ability and 100 per cent effort. When Dave goes for a ball, he usually gets it! And when you remember that *twice* he has come back from breaking a leg, it says much for his courage and determination.

Come down to around the 5 foot 7 inch mark now, and what do we see? – full-backs Tony Dunne (Manchester United), Joe Kinnear (Tottenham) and Bernard Shaw (Sheffield United). It would be hard to find better players in English Soccer for their positions.

Move forward, and there are wing-halves Brian O'Neil (Burnley) and John Hollins (Chelsea); forwards George Eastham (Stoke), Ian St. John (Liverpool), Alex Young (Everton) and Jimmy Melia (Southampton). All these players have gained representative honours.

We'll drop the measuring rod still further, to around the 5 foot 6 inch mark, and bring in Billy Bremner (Leeds) and Colin Harvey (Everton), both wing-halves who have stamped the game with their skill and authority. And no-one can question Billy Bremner's ability to dispute a fifty-fifty ball with anyone!

Even smaller is my England buddy, Nobby Stiles, of Manchester United. They call Nobby 'Happy' at Old Trafford – but on the field, as opponents well know, he's tigerish in the tackle, and he reads a game tremendously well. Move over to Leeds again, and there you'll find inside-forward Johnny Giles . . the brother-in-law of Nobby Stiles.

Perhaps there's half an inch difference in height between Johnny and Nobby – with Nobby that shade taller. And it's worth recalling that not so long ago, when I picked my top team of world players, I included Nobby Stiles and Ray Wilson. I don't think there would be many arguments about that, either.

Still not satisfied? Then what about Willie Carlin, the inside-forward who was transferred from Carlisle to Sheffield United for £40,000? That may not be a world-record fee, but it was big money for the Blades to pay out . . . and I reckon Willie must be a classic case to prove my point.

He's a Liverpool lad who was allowed to leave Merseyside; he cost Carlisle a chicken-feed fee when they signed him from Halifax; and he was the 'general' who inspired Carlisle's rise up into the Second Division.

I am told, indeed, that while Willie was with Carlisle, he was watched for quite a time by a First Division club who thought he had the skill which they were seeking . . . but, finally, they decided that he wasn't quite big enough. But with Carlisle and with Sheffield United, Willie Carlin has certainly proved that he is *good* enough.

My final example is a player who is now with Bury, but who started his career with Glasgow Celtic, moved down to Everton, and then on to Leeds. Yes, I mean Bobby Collins, at about 5 foot $3\frac{1}{2}$ inches a pocket-sized general, if ever there was one.

17

'Here is a wing-half famed and feared for his ability and one hundred per cent effort' – Spurs' Dave Mackay contorts in mid-air under challenge from Birmingham left-back Green.

He cost Everton something like £25,000 when he arrived from Celtic – and he became the uncrowned 'king' of Goodison. After several seasons of great service, he moved on to Leeds – and Everton recouped every penny of the fee they had paid Celtic for him.

Bobby helped to steer Leeds away from the peril of plunging into the *Third* Division, played a significant part in their rise up the *Second* Division table, and was a source of inspiration in their promotion season and in their magnificent run of success in the *First* Division.

He helped to steer Leeds to the First Division runners-up spot, to an F.A. Cup Final at Wembley, and into Europe. He was named Footballer of the Year, and was recalled to the Scotland team. He broke a leg playing in the white-hot cauldron of European Soccer, fought his way back to fitness . . .

and moved on to Bury to help stage another rescue act, as the Gigg Lane club sought to bounce back to the Second Division.

Almost all the players I have mentioned have won international honours with England, Scotland or the Republic of Ireland. In every case, like myself, they have had to overcome the so-called disadvantage of lacking height in their respective positions. And, like me, no doubt they have had to tell themselves at times: 'The bigger they are, the harder they fall!'

So to any lad who may have heard those words which I once heard . . . 'He's not big enough' . . . I would say this: 'Remember it isn't always size which makes a would-be footballer a good footballer. It's ability, determination and effort. In short, ability plus 100 per cent dedication. If you've got the ability, and you are determined enough, you *can* reach the top.'

More cheers for the little 'uns! – FACING PAGE, TOP, *Sunderland's tiny terror Bobby Kerr heads home the first of two goals against Newcastle;* BELOW, *Sunderland inside man John O'Hare has Everton 'keeper Gordon West at sixes and sevens.* THIS PAGE, BELOW, *it's Alan Ball in terrific action again, scoring an only goal to beat Liverpool in a Merseyside 'derby'.*

WILLIE HENDERSON

THERE can never have been a happier – nor a prouder – wee Ranger than I am. I'm delighted I joined the Light Blues, delighted my father chased off the English club who offered him a dining-room suite for my 'autograph' when I was still a schoolboy. . . .

But a couple of things annoy me just the same!

First, the sneerers who've written and even phoned when I've been injured – and it would surprise you how many abusive communications footballers get – accusing me of being in no hurry to get back into the team.

It's a load of old rubbish.

When I've been out of action through injury, and I've had my share of idle time, I'm desperate to get back into the game. So desperate I can't sit still and watch. 'You'll blow a fuse, Willie, if you don't stop jumping up and down,' Davy Wilson once told me when we were both crocked and in the stand.

DON'T OVERWORK
THE THEORIES . . . .

While football's been good to me, I've had my share of the bad luck. Take a look at my catalogue of misfortunes over the last few years:

1964: Broken nose for third time. 1965: Bunion operation; torn ankle ligaments. 1966: Strained thigh muscles. 1967: Broken jaw; cartilage operation.

You wouldn't say I was the luckiest player in the game – although you have to take the good with the bad.

My second dislike is what I think of as football geometry. You know what I mean – the game reduced to so many angles and theorems. I believe, indeed, there's far too much off-the-field theorising nowadays.

As a player, and I like to think a ball player, I'm

by WILLIE HENDERSON
(Rangers and Scotland)

convinced pre-arranged strategies and theories can be overdone. General tactics, yes. You've got to figure out in advance, I know, what sort of game to play as a team, how to cope with the opposition's strong points, and so on.

But I know, too, that if I had to try to concentrate on specific moves, moves designed for me individually, I'd never beat my man and get the ball across. And that, after all, is why I'm playing for Rangers . . . and proud to be playing for Rangers.

It was as a Ranger, however, a very new Ranger at that, that I had my most embarrassing moment in football – or to be more precise, in a restaurant.

We were leaving the restaurant, one of Edinburgh's classier eateries, when the manager asked me, but politely, if I'd mind opening my football bag – and made it clear he didn't mind whether I minded or not.

I demanded to know why, in a squeak I tried vainly to make sound like thunder. But I opened the bag just the same . . . and found out why. In addition to my football gear, it was stuffed full of the restaurant's cutlery.

My team-mates had decided to pull a fast one on the '*wee yin*', had bunged the loot in my bag while my attention was distracted, and had arranged with another customer to tip off the manager. He took a bit of convincing that we were in fact the Rangers and the whole thing was a joke.

I've 'won' a good few mementoes in the way of caps and medals, of course, during my years at Ibrox. But always legitimately!

Surely a goal for Rangers? – but no, Orjan Persson looses his shot (LEFT) *from the six-yards line and through a grounded Clyde defence . . . but misses.* RIGHT, *Rangers 'keeper Erik Sorenson with a facial expression fellow goalkeepers will understand – he's watching a header from Hibs'*
Pat Quinn very anxiously indeed, but it was over the bar . . .

It's one of my few pre-match strategies to try to stick to playing football no matter what happens. But believe me it's difficult, mighty difficult, to keep your head if you're spending more time on the deck than you are on the ball.

I've been chopped down so often I've felt it was hardly worth while getting up. I've even felt like doing something about it . . . but when you're my height and weight, fisticuffs are very much a last resort.

Yet I did take a poke at an opponent on one occasion.

That was against Seville in a European cup-tie in Spain in 1962, and the bloke I punched was the Spanish goalkeeper. He was asking for it in such a big way even wee Willie couldn't refuse.

Scots awa'! – LEFT, TOP, it's Northern Ireland's Derek Dougan going for a high ball closely attended by Scotland's Ure and McKinnon; BELOW, Johnny Crossan takes a penalty for the Irish but Scotland's Ronnie Simpson makes a sensational save, and, INSET, Simpson in not-so-happy mood, burying his face in his hands as the Scots make a bad miss at the other end! ABOVE, Rangers' Willie Johnston walks off with a big smile – he's just shattered Morton with a two-minute goal; RIGHT, it's Scotland's Ure-McKinnon team again, this time beating off an Irish raid.

It was a punch which started a riot, however. Seville strong man Canario, right-winger in the famous Real Madrid side who beat Eintracht in that never-to-be-forgotten European Cup Final at Hampden, came at me like he was a wild bull – and I was a matador's cape.

I got out of his way, however, with a bit of foot-work any matador would have been proud of . . . but, the crowd roaring him on, he came at me again and again, and would almost certainly have caught me if Bobby Shearer and Billy Ritchie hadn't made it clear they were on my side.

The Continentals apart, and they can get on with the game quite easily without the ball, particularly if they're losing, I can remember only one occasion when violence was literally staring me in the face – although I didn't realise it at the time.

I thought the full-back was joking when he threatened that if I tried to beat him on the outside he'd *'stoat me aff the terracing wall'*. But he wasn't, as I found out.

It happened in a reserve game before I made the Rangers big team. I'd been having one of my better days, cutting inside and taking the ball in on goal. Then, having forgotten the threat to *'stoat'* me, I took the outside of the full-back . . . and the next thing I knew I was lying flat out on the track with the trainer telling me not to move until he'd checked if I'd broken any bones.

I hadn't, but walking was agony. Even nodding my head was an effort for the next few days.

There was one occasion, however, when Ralph Brand couldn't walk at all. Ralph, who had to travel to Edinburgh, was always one of the first into 'civvies' and off his mark after training – a fact the Ibrox practical jokers hadn't missed.

So when he stepped into his moccasin-type shoes one day and shouted 'Cheerio', he promptly fell flat on his face. Two of the boys had nailed the shoes to the floor – and told the rest of us. We were all waiting, therefore, for Ralph to make his big exit.

It was funnier by a mile, from where I sat at any rate, than the time when Jim Baxter and company pulled off my shoes, threw them out of the window of a Monaco hotel, and stood looking down as I tried to get them back from the local in the street who thought they were the modern form of manna.

Aye, it's a great game. And it's been a good game to me in many, many ways. Not only have I seen European playgrounds like Monaco first-class, toured America and even been to Russia, I've a splendid home on the outskirts of Glasgow and am a lot better known than if I'd been a butcher, a baker or a candlestick-maker.

And while it's true that the butchers, the bakers and the candlestick-makers are a lot less liable than I am to finish up limping after a day's work, don't forget the game is bound to get tougher as the rewards get higher.

With 'Continental' bonuses at stake, it can be as hard to lose as it is to win. That's human nature.

THE THIRD MAN

IFB EDITORIAL

- **FOR FIFTEEN YEARS** the football world has puzzled over the 'missing link', the element of telepathy which seemed to put the final stamp on the pre-1954 Hungarians, greatest team the world has yet seen.
  IN THE LAST YEAR a Europe-wide inquiry has pieced together a number of clues to describe what can now be called 'The Third Man Theory' – which only West Ham among British teams seem to have pursued. . . .
- **DR. GEZA KALOCSAI,** one of the coaches who built Hungary's greatness, told us: 'If you were the manager of a First Division team you would never permit your article to be published . . . but use it to win the Championship.'
  BRITISH FOOTBALL has clearly recovered much of the prestige lost back in 1953–54, but this Inquiry is still vitally relevant, because it is concerned with quality and not achievement.

THERE is a good reason why West Ham, despite normal ups and downs of form, are one of the most liked teams in the country. There is an essential element in their good, attacking football which – if no longer 'Secret' – remains 'Strictly Confidential'.

Only now, after fourteen years of inquiries, can that essential element be described. And with that is broken a long conspiracy of silence between the world's top coaches – men who are naturally out to protect salaries running up to £40,000 a year.

Men like Helenio Herrera of Inter., Bela Guttmann of Benfica and many others, Albert Batteaux of France . . . and Ron Greenwood of West Ham. They are all 'in the know'.

West Ham are the only British team to offer evidence over a period that they have linked to this vital 'Third Man Theory'. On the pattern elsewhere, it would therefore seem safe to predict that West Ham will win not one but *several* Football League Championships in the next few years.

Is that unbelievable in view, for example, of West Ham's present League position? Well, you'll perhaps recall that England drew 0–0 with Uruguay in the World Cup and that the forward line was Ball, Greaves, Charlton, Hunt and Connelly.

For the Final Hurst replaced Greaves and Peters replaced Connelly. Hurst scored three, Peters one: both West Ham players. But just as important B.B.C. monitor microphones around the pitch picked up something interesting.

More often than not it was the West Ham men in England's World Cup-winning team who were *directing the running off the ball by their team mates.*

To an expert listener the on-field calling would suggest one thing: the West Ham men were putting into effect what they have learned and are continuing to learn about the Third Man Theory.

In fact, to such an expert, it would have followed that Ron Greenwood also deserved credit for his indirect but decisive contribution to England's World Cup success – a contribution which began four years ago, when Greenwood first began following through on his own insight into the Theory.

Little wonder Henderson, in background, looks thrilled by this Roger Hynd goal – it's a second for Rangers against Celtic, and that's something to be specially thrilled about . . . if you're a Ranger!

ANOTHER underlining of its importance came during an interview with beatle-browed Dr. Geza Kalocsai, the formidable Hungarian manager of Polish champions Gornik Zabrze. He said:

'If you were the manager of a First Division team you would never permit your article to be published. You would not tell anyone what you knew, but would use it to win the Championship.'

Dr. Kalocsai knows. A lawyer by training, he became one of the three coaches under the astute Gustav Sebes who prepared the most gifted all-round team the world has so far seen: the pre-1954 Hungarians.

The other two were Martin Bukovi, now manager of Olympiakos, champions of Greece, and Janos Kalmar. Kalmar coaches Espanol, a poor and un-fashionable club in Barcelona which nevertheless, with a young and untried team, finished third last season behind millionaire clubs Real Madrid and C.F. Barcelona.

It is no accident that these three men carry success around the Continent with them. They are the original creators and guardians of the Third Man Theory, which is nothing less than this:

The revolutionary idea – the elusive 'difference' which has worried the world's football critics for

Flashback (RIGHT) *to November 25, 1953. Wembley: England 3, Hungary 6. Stan Mortensen takes a flier over 'keeper Gyula Grosics, who's gathered the ball safely: 'The Hungarian ideas were mis-interpreted.'*

years – which linked and motivated the great Hungarian team that smashed England 6–3 at Wembley and 7–1 in Budapest.

But like the Third Man of films, their theory has been a long-running fugitive. Not least because none of the handful of people 'in the know' were prepared, at least until now, to open up on the subject.

Similarly, when they won the leadership of world football at Wembley in 1953 it must have given the Hungarians a certain grim satisfaction to have had their ideas so generally misinterpreted abroad, and they did nothing to alter that situation.

At the time the Hungarians drew comments like, 'They played like men from another planet', and 'If this was football, then what is the game we've been playing in England for the last thirty years'.

For a long series of games both before, during and after the 1954 World Cup the Hungarians' moves were charted and analysed. But with one fatal fault: only the movements of the ball were noted. In general, it is true of all ball games, tennis being an example, that nobody watches the man running off the ball.

Martin Bukovi (TOP) – *'He first developed the Third Man Theory.'* BELOW, *Hungarian players jog along with – second from right, coach Janos Kalmar: 'The truth is, people didn't see what we were doing in training. . . .'*

WING COMMANDER Charles Reep, an innovator of football charts, worked closely with Wolves on a breakdown of what made

Hungary tick. In a nutshell, they decided it was 'the long pass which brings goals'.

It proved only one piece of the jigsaw, and by no means the most significant – but it was enough to win Wolves an English Championship or two. But it was not enough when they came up against top European competition, particularly Barcelona, then managed by Herrera.

Another idea current in Britain was that the Hungarians played just another form of Arthur Rowe's 'push and run' game which won Spurs the 1950 and 1951 Championships. This proves to have been much closer to the mark than any other theory.

What was missed is that something had been *added* to Rowe's plan – and it was that something which has eluded most of the game's thinkers ever since.

In his time Rowe was one of the few experts aware of the vital relationship between man and ball. Invited to lecture in Hungary, Rowe saw the beginnings, but only the beginnings, of the new Hungarian game.

It was simply, push the ball and run into space – looking for a return pass. Not till three years later, in 1950, did the Hungarians add an extra twist to this basic theme. But in the interim, what Rowe had learned was enough to set up Spurs in the top (English) class.

As Hungary rose to her zenith only a handful of experienced coaches were able to spot just what the Hungarians were doing. But those who did were very careful to keep their observations to themselves; it was in their professional interest to do so.

The coaches' attitude of 'Why should we reveal our secrets?' is, after all, just as prevalent in Britain. Here, only Walter Winterbottom was prepared to put what he knew into print, but even so his generosity often backfired.

The late Jack Shreeve, former Charlton Athletic coach, summed up the wariness of the best British coaches. He said: 'I go to Lilleshall every year for the coaching conference.

'Walter is the driving force there, but his attempts to develop unity amongst the coaches fail completely. We all go to learn but nobody is prepared to give anything to the conference.

'If we've found something good, given an extra twist to a basic idea which everyone knows, we keep it to ourselves. You see, it became clear that if we revealed all we knew it would be incorporated in the F.A.'s next coaching book and everyone would get what we knew for nothing.'

IN researching for this article a similar personal outlook was discovered almost everywhere. Well-known coaches will talk freely up to a point. But they decline to add anything which the questioner does not already know, nor which is not common knowledge.

Take Herrera. At the Inter. training ground at Appiano Gentile forty miles from Milan a high wire fence keeps out Press, strangers and spies. Security guards are posted at the main gate. No one gets in without a pass signed by Herrera.

So how Herrera prepares his team remains a secret. Public workouts when travelling abroad are limited to physical preparations and static-ball practice. How Inter. train is the key to the way they play, as it is for every team.

But that training is secret in its most essential phases.

Similarly, in several lengthy conversations, Herrera refused to be drawn on the really important questions. He will explain that the 'free back' is necessary because the centre-half is alone and can be easily drawn out of position. But when asked *how* the free back can be drawn out he becomes vague and evasive.

He knows. But he isn't saying.

Nandor Hidegkuti, centre-forward in the great Hungarian side, and now a coach, is likewise reluctant to part with knowledge. He said: 'More intelligent people are thinking about the game today than ever before. But the more they think the worse the game becomes. The trouble is they are thinking only about defence and we must think in terms of developing our play in attack.'

Pressed to develop this topic Hidegkuti also became vague.

With a shrug he said: 'It's difficult . . . we must have skilful and intelligent players and they are not easy to find these days.' But one can be sure that Hidegkuti's success as a coach does not depend on the lottery of whether or not he has good players with whom to work.

Hidegkuti was at the very centre of the Third Man Theory, and must know its significance well.

Triumph continues

THESE men know. So did Albert Batteaux, a sophisticated French coach – dark, of medium height, always impeccably dressed. Batteaux was a student through the early '50s of the Hungarian team and his sharp nose similarly sniffed out the vital element.

He managed Rheims, whose home gates averaged around 7,000, but with the backing of champagne millionaire Henri Germain he developed seven players for the French National team, whom he coached to the semi-final of the 1958 World Cup, much to the world's surprise.

Batteaux now manages St. Étienne, who were previously managed by his 1958 World Cup assistant, Jean Snella. St. Étienne are the French champions. The Third Man Theory continues triumphant!

In fact it is more alive at second hand – in the minds of Europe's leading coaches – than it is in its place of origin, Budapest. Ironically, Budapest has mislaid its inheritence.

The reasons are all too familiar.

In Hungary it is the men of political power who have the last word, just as in England it is the prerogative of the men who put up the money. Ujpest, for instance. It is the club of the Police and prisoners weed the pitch under armed guard. The (active) President is the Chief of Police.

After the shock of the 1954 World Cup Final defeat by West Germany, Hungary's team boss Gustav Sebes was retired – a political decision. He is now inactive in Tatabanya, a town some 40 miles from Budapest. With him went most of the driving force behind Hungary's rapid climb to world dominance.

Then came 1956, the Revolution – and the departure of Puskas, Kocsis and Czibor, somewhat hurriedly. But equally important the 18-strong Hungarian Youth squad – her team of the future – was touring England at the time. Few of them returned home.

In Budapest now, there is less evidence of the political regime. The depressing red stars over public buildings along the Danube appear fewer. But there is even less evidence of the pre-1954 football glory.

Three games were studied for the purpose of this article: Ferencvaros v. Honved, Vasas v. Csepel and Ujpest v. Diosgyor. In each game one of Hungary's top current national stars appeared – Florian Albert, Janos Farkas and Ferenc Bene.

Without exception the games followed strict-formation *catenaccio,* the Italian game based on 1–4–2–3. No player comes from behind. Everyone plays to stop the opposition scoring.

The Hungarians have forgotten, more probably no longer know, because of the folly of sacking their football leadership in 1954 and cramping the style of the disheartened few who remained in office.

Checked by a conspiracy of silence among the coaches, plus a Budapest out of touch with its own creation, how then was the Third Man Theory

Rudolf Nureyev? – No, just plain ol' Charlie Cooke of Chelsea leaping mightily to beat West Ham's earthbound John Charles, left.

tracked down? How could the element in Hungary's greatness which has defied analysis for fourteen years begin to be defined?

Luck – and at last, knowing what the right questions were and to whom to put them.

THE first real break in the search for Hungary's Third Man Theory – the element which pulled every other factor together to make her, before 1954, the greatest team the world has so far seen – was given by Bela Guttmann.

Guttmann, himself Hungarian-born, is the man who discovered and developed Eusebio and many other good players, the man who has coached half the top clubs in Europe, or so it has seemed.

In a first interview Guttmann confined himself to areas of common knowledge, talking freely. But when the conversation turned to the problems of playing against deep, Italian-style defences he, too, became vague and evasive.

'An instinct for football is important,' he said. 'Without it no coach can be successful. Developing young players is like cutting diamonds, shaving a piece here, a touch there.

'You take a young player and aim to emphasise his strong points and polish up his failings to make him as close to being the complete player as you can.'

But when Guttmann, the grand old man of European coaching, came to England for the World Cup it was as a spectator. He was already semi-retired – and disguised by heavy dark glasses.

This time he admitted that those who knew the secrets of football kept them strictly to themselves. Then, rather excitingly, he said: 'I will show you everything.'

Then he added: 'But I cannot let you see *with my eyes.*'

Guttmann did get a new team – Swiss Cup-holders Servette, of Geneva. But before the season was ended Servette and Bela Guttmann had, disappointingly, parted company.

Still, Guttmann had said something else which was soon to become ringingly significant. 'Part of the secret,' he said, 'is having players running off the ball to create space, but it's difficult to explain. It's better to show you in practice.'

THE phrase 'running off the ball' is not, of course, new. But equally it has never been satisfactorily defined – even by F.A. coaches who recognise its value, but don't really know how to get it.

LEFT, *Denis Law plays piggy-back with a Hibernians-Malta defender in Manchester United's European Cup game.* FACING PAGE, TOP, *West Ham and England skipper Bobby Moore keeps Chelsea's Boyle under firm control;* BELOW, *dynamic Geoff Hurst, Moore's West Ham and England team-mate, escapes with the ball from a scything tackle by Chelsea's Ron Harris.*

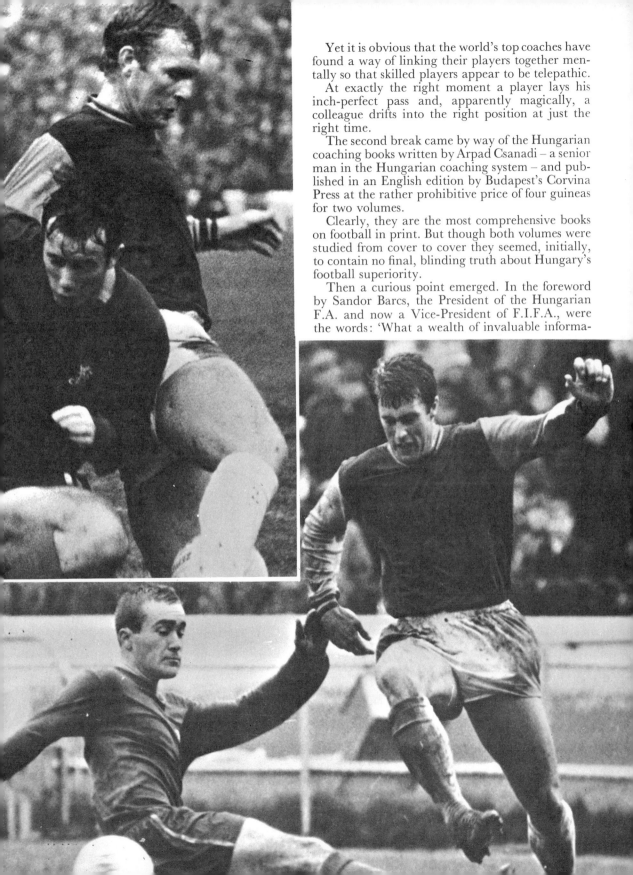

Yet it is obvious that the world's top coaches have found a way of linking their players together mentally so that skilled players appear to be telepathic.

At exactly the right moment a player lays his inch-perfect pass and, apparently magically, a colleague drifts into the right position at just the right time.

The second break came by way of the Hungarian coaching books written by Arpad Csanadi – a senior man in the Hungarian coaching system – and published in an English edition by Budapest's Corvina Press at the rather prohibitive price of four guineas for two volumes.

Clearly, they are the most comprehensive books on football in print. But though both volumes were studied from cover to cover they seemed, initially, to contain no final, blinding truth about Hungary's football superiority.

Then a curious point emerged. In the foreword by Sandor Barcs, the President of the Hungarian F.A. and now a Vice-President of F.I.F.A., were the words: 'What a wealth of invaluable information and observation is given on the systems, tactics and coaching – all of which are covered in the second and third volumes.'

The point which finally registered was that only the first *two* volumes have been translated into English. Presumably the Hungarians have retained the contents of volume three for themselves.

But in Budapest another possibility arose, that volume three, though probably drafted, was never in fact published. Dr. Kalocsai, now in Poland, edited the first two volumes for technical accuracy, but said nothing about the third.

The missing volume is still a puzzle. But in a conversation, Ron Greenwood was unconvinced that it existed at all. 'It's not needed, anyway,' he said enigmatically. 'It's all in the two published books *if you can recognise it*.'

His words were similar to those earlier words of Guttmann's – 'I cannot let you see it with my eyes.'

Clearly the Hungarian books had to be studied again, but this time trying to read them with the eyes of Greenwood and Guttmann.

THIS, obviously, is difficult. In football as in anything else, to accept everything at face value is to miss the vital point. Two football fans could watch exactly the same training at two different clubs and not realise that the purposes of the training were quite different.

At Arsenal one could see the players sprinting in pairs over 40 yards. At Tottenham the other could see exactly the same – players sprinting over 40 yards in pairs. Both might assume that both clubs were after speed, general fitness and stamina.

But to know for sure, the periods of rest between each sprint must be timed. If the rest periods are short then the player will tire quickly and cannot possibly improve his speed because of growing

The ball looks as if it's through Pat Jennings' hands – but the Northern Ireland goalkeeper held this shot, a cracker!, from England's Roger Hunt.

fatigue.

But if lengthy rest periods are allowed, so that the player can fully recover before the next dash, then improved speed will be the objective. Some thought must be given before the 'hidden purpose' of any practice can be accurately seen.

So by pondering each Hungarian exercise and asking, 'What is the purpose of this?' and 'Exactly what are the players doing here?' a simple fundamental truth of Soccer came out: the key to the Hungarian ability to produce world-class players from ball practice alone.

There are a whole series of ball practices with an ingredient not 'seen' before. For instance, a heading practice in which the players stand in a circle: A begins by heading the ball to B *and then running to take the place of B*; then B heads the ball to, say, E *and runs to take the place of E*.

Yet another exercise, ostensibly for trapping and passing, had this same ingredient. The players were all changing places with the man to whom they passed or headed the ball.

Similarly, in a section headed 'Compound forms of attack', there were exercises designed, apparently, to develop ball skill. For two, then three players – but in each case passing combined with place changing.

POSITIONAL SWITCHING, ONCE THOUGHT TO BE A HAPHAZARD ELEMENT, BROUGHT TO A DISCIPLINED ART.

RUNNING TO TAKE THE PLACE OF THE MAN TO WHOM THE PLAYER HAS PASSED.

A SIMPLE YET EFFECTIVE METHOD OF LINKING ALL THE PLAYERS TOGETHER.

THE ONLY ACCURATE WAY OF IMPLEMENTING THE 'WHIRL' FORECAST TWELVE YEARS AGO BY WILLY MEISL IN THE WEST BUT ALREADY 'IN PRODUCTION' BY THE HUNGARIANS IN THE EAST. . . .

THINK in terms of the Hungarians at Wembley in 1953. Time and again Sandor Kocsis and Ferenc Puskas broke through the centre with England centre-half Harry Johnston nowhere to be seen.

Changing places with the man to whom the player passes the ball leads inevitably to the 'Whirl'. If the right-half gives the ball to the outside-right then he must run to outside-right. Seven gives to four (now outside-right) and runs to the right wing.

Now where is the opposing left-back? He might have followed seven to centre-forward in which case there is no real and effective left-back. Or he might

33

Another fine shot of Bobby Charlton – breaking at speed through the Wales' defence.

have remained in position and is now marking four. But in that case who is marking seven – the new centre-forward?

There is the secret which fixed Harry Johnston at Wembley and Luton's Sid Owen in Budapest. At centre-half they had to mark up to five or six men because any player who gave the ball to Hidegkuti automatically raced to centre-forward and was unmarked.

Update this idea to the West Ham of today. Left-back John Charles passes up to left-winger John Sissons. Sissons moves inside with the ball (screened from the full-back) towards Geoff Hurst, taking the full-back with him. Once inside, Sissons plays the ball to Ron Boyce at inside-right. Boyce puts the ball over the heads of the defenders to the left wing – where there is not Sissons, but Charles. Charles is the 'Third Man', the 'one put in from behind' – not occasionally or accidentally, but as a matter of training and habit.

There is the simple idea which passed for 'telepathy' in the Hungarians of 1953 and which only a handful of Europe's leading coaches identified and acted upon in the fifteen years since; and which has continued to worry so many more.

For confirmation that this was, indeed, the 'missing link' Dr. Geza Kalocsai – one of the three coaches who worked under Sebes to build Hungary – was again approached in Poland. A broad-shouldered tough man with a piercing eye, in his middle fifties, he cracked:

'Now you know the right questions you'll get the right answers.'

Bukovi the first

TO start, he stopped the Gornik training session and asked ten of his players to form a rectangle. The man with the ball could pass to anyone he liked, but he had to run to take that man's place – even while that man was making a similar pass to another.

As an aside, he said: 'If you ask players to do twenty-yard sprints they go mad. With this sort of exercise they do the sprints anyway, and enjoy it. People used to say the Hungarians didn't do traditional training, only training with the ball – the truth is, those people didn't *see* what we were doing. . . .'

KALOCSAI confirmed that the basis of this article was the line on which the Hungarians were coached. Under Sebes these men did the actual coaching – Martin Bukovi, Janos Kalmar and Kalocsai himself.

Bukovi, he said, was the man who first developed the Third Man Theory. Around 1950 Bukovi began to feel that a high degree of technical skill was not enough. 'We needed a method of creating collectivity – making individual players think and move as a unit.'

Kalocsai went on: 'What we called combinations were the result of this, with the ordinary wall-pass the starting point. With the wall-pass we linked two men together, but we soon realised that this was easily spotted: the two players completed their move in full view of the defender.

'Again it was Bukovi who introduced the Third Man to make a basic one-two-three, with the third man coming from behind and running into a position on the "blind side" of the defender.

'After that it all fell naturally into place. We developed more and more of these basic combinations, linking groups of three and then four players together. After many months of practice it was clear that players were moving and thinking as one attacking unit.

'Coaching this way is not easy. It's far more difficult than coaching ball skills. But it's also more interesting, for both coach and players. Intelligence is now the vital feature in the make-up of a player, though naturally the greatest coach can do little for a player lacking in talent.'

The tragedy for British football – even allowing England's World Cup triumph and Celtic's memorable European Cup win – is that we took combination play little further than the wall-pass. Asked why the Third Man Theory had not been analysed and taught on F.A. courses, a senior coach said caustically: 'They didn't know!'

Now Europe's conspiracy of silence has been broken and the idea is there for all to act. The Third Man Theory could revolutionise football thinking in Britain.

34

Manchester City – last season's most dramatically improved club team - in action against Wolves. TOP, *it's Neil Young going high to score a real eye-catcher and,* BELOW, *Francis Lee, City's big signing from Bolton forces past Wolves' Bobby Thomson to get in a shot.*

MEET THE BALL —AND ATTACK!

by JANOS FARKAS

(Vasas Budapest and Hungary)

I WAS only a boy playing for the Laszlo Hospital Club in a local league when the great Hungarian team of 1950–55 was at its best. I saw the great players often – Puskas, Kocsis, Hidegkuti – each of them a master in his own right. And as I remember them, theirs was the kind of football I would like to play.

Nowadays, of course, it isn't so easy to play real football because everyone seems to be copying the F.C. Internazionale style of play. I've played against Inter. twice and didn't enjoy the experience. I've also watched them on several other occasions . . . without enjoying it.

The players who help make the defensive system work can't enjoy it either and I'm sure the public doesn't like it. Given the choice, the fans would always prefer the open, attacking football on which I was brought up. The modern defensive game chokes the players' ability and eliminates all the natural beauty in football.

I like to win games as much as anyone, but playing good football and scoring goals are just as important to me as winning. Not being a coach, and not having given much thought to the theory of the game, I don't see an easy answer. But there are a few things I have learned which help to beat *catenaccio*-type defences.

The most important is going to meet the ball, rather than waiting for it to come to you. In tight-marking games where a particular player has been detailed to shadow me, I've learned that speed off the mark – suddenly sprinting to meet a pass – has shaken off everyone.

Another thing I'm sure about is the value of positional switching which certainly upsets most defences when the changes are effected quickly.

The Hungarian team of the early 1950s were really great at this, and I'm sure they would beat the Inter.-type defences. Maybe they wouldn't score six or seven goals a

36

Remember that great Farkas goal against Brazil at Liverpool? – Just to prove he doesn't need a World Cup to bring the best out of him Farkas here scores an equally dramatic goal in a Hungarian club match.

game as they often did in their heyday but they would score often enough to win.

Portuguese champions Benfica have come closest to this extremely high standard in my experience, and at times the Hungarian team in which I played in the 1966 World Cup was also very good. Most of that team is young enough to play again in Mexico, and with the changes we are making in Hungary I'm optimistic about our chances in 1970.

No one will argue that Hungarian football is not amongst the best in the world. Like everyone else our standards have varied from time to time, but generally the Hungarians are usually amongst the top half-dozen countries.

In the 1966 World Cup – which was my first series – we were excellent against Brazil, but in the match with Russia some of our deficiencies were exposed. Based on those experiences our coaches have changed our training patterns to improve general condition and other physical qualities.

Traditionally the Hungarian game has been based on skill rather than strength and stamina. The players prefer it this way, and the fans have always idolised the ball players. Things are changing a little in this respect but not enough as yet.

In Hungarian League matches for example the fans like their team to win, but not simply by scoring more goals than the opposition. They want their favourites to dribble round opponents, and then bring the ball back and do it again!

When it comes to international matches at club or representative level the emphasis changes considerably. Now the Hungarian fans will be satisfied with victory, and experience has shown that beating teams like England, Russia, West Germany and a few others demands not only clever players but a blend of ability with 'fighting football'.

The fans can't have it both ways. Now they must accept and encourage a greater degree of determination in our domestic football and applaud the straight-for-goal type of move.

As a spectator I quite like the English-type football, though I think I'd get bored with it after a while if I saw the same kind of game each week. I find it interesting playing against British teams too; interesting, but not enjoyable.

I look forward to meeting England here in Budapest, where I think the conditions would suit us more than Wembley. I'd also like to nominate the referee for this match: the Italian Signor Lo Bello is the man for me – strict, but honest and objective.

Many referees certainly help teams like England and Russia by allowing defenders to use their bodies rather than their brains. I never mind hard tackling as long as the defender is making a real attempt to kick the ball, but too often defenders are trying only to kick my legs. A good referee can see the difference.

Generally, we are now working towards a marriage of the Hungarian style of football and the more physical game played by England, West Germany and Russia. It isn't easy for the players, who until now have usually done all their training with the ball. But given time I'm sure it will be successful.

Obviously a switch to professionalism would be a big step in this direction, for at the moment we have to do a job outside football and train as well. Some teams train in the evenings after work but most, like Vasas, train in the afternoons. It isn't easy coming from work to train, and professionals obviously have advantages, with nothing else to make demands on their minds and their energy.

Scotland beat England at Wembley – Jim McCalliog's first appearance for Scotland, and here he's congratulated by fellow debutant Ronnie Simpson (left).

MY FIRST HUNDRED THOUSAND

(miles, that is...)

by JIM McCALLIOG

(Sheffield Wednesday and Scotland)

ALAN BROWN, our former manager at Hillsborough, was a great believer in foreign travel. It broadens the mind, he said, both generally and football-wise.

No one could qualify for a diploma from the boss's Soccer academy unless he had been tried and tested under the conditions of football abroad, against players of differing temperaments and skill, and in front of crowds even more fanatical than those at Anfield and Old Trafford.

If the boss was right – and to be fair to him, he nearly always was – I should be just about the best player who ever pulled on a football boot 'in anger'!

I am only a few months past my 21st birthday, but I have already travelled over 100,000 miles on the Soccer beat in the few years since I left my native Glasgow.

When Alan Brown bought me from Chelsea, there were plenty of folk who thought he was taking a terrific gamble forking out a big fee for a 17-year-old stripling who had only seven League games under his belt.

That was the number quoted – and it was correct. But what he also knew was that I had made well over thirty appearances for Tommy Docherty's side – nine on a ten-game tour of Australia, as well as turning out in other senior games in Sweden, Germany, Switzerland, Denmark and Austria on pre-season trips.

I had also been abroad with the Scottish Youth team for a Mini-World Cup tournament in Holland and had been a member of a London Youth side which played the youth of France in an annual game in Paris.

In fact, I have often wondered if Mr. Brown was not more impressed by my record of foreign travel and experience than he was by my ability when he persuaded me to leave Stamford Bridge for Sheffield!

Since I have been at Hillsborough, we have shown our paces in such far-off places as Hong Kong, Malaysia, Singapore and Bulgaria. It was only because I was a member of a Scottish F.A. party which toured Israel, Hong Kong (again), Australia (once more), Canada and New Zealand which

'English football is the toughest and best in the world,' says much-travelled Jim McCalliog. Here, Sheffield Wednesday team-mate Vic Mobley makes a fine picture as he tries a header – against some pretty determined Southampton opposition.

stopped me adding Mexico to my list with Wednesday.

Altogether, I think I have been at least a couple of times round the world and have been able to study the set-up at first hand in well over a dozen countries.

The conclusions I have reached are that English football is the toughest and the best in the world and that players, with very few exceptions, do not come any better than Britain has produced in the last decade.

Still, the greatest player I have seen is Alfredo di Stefano. Since the first time I saw him play I have been mesmerised by his all-round brilliance. Certainly, he is the type of player I would like to be – and nobody is going to stop me trying!

He has everything, in my opinion, and would have been a shining star in any country, any team, any era. He was worth every peseta of the fabulous money he was reckoned to be earning by dedicating himself to the game.

Now that the abolition of the maximum wage has put us on our mettle, I believe the British professional has become the most proficient and dedicated in the world. And with managers like Alan Brown, Sir Alf Ramsey, Jock Stein, Don Revie and Bill Shankly around to set the standards and keep us on the right track, I believe we are going to get better.

These men know exactly what they want. They see that they get it, too. Unlike some of their predecessors they can see that a new idea is not necessarily the 'bee's knees' just because it comes from the Continent or South America.

They are always willing to look and listen. But then they analyse, adapt – even improve. All the old hide-bound thinking and ideas have been discarded and now we are technically right out in front.

But anyone who believes it is going to be easy to stay there had better think again.

We McCalliogs have always been a Soccer-mad family. One of the things I remember from my very young days was how the 'auld folks' were shaken to the core by the news that Hungary had dared to come to Wembley and trounce England out of sight.

It did not seem possible that a team which had given Scotland a convincing beating the same season could have let a bunch of 'foreigners' knock them off their pedestal!

British football will never again become complacent, of that I am certain.

Now that's not very nice, is it? – Sheffield Wednesday's Jack Whitham looks somewhat pained (LEFT) as he's brought down from behind by Chelsea's Marvin Hinton. RIGHT, an equally unpleasant moment for Wednesday – 'keeper Peter Springett is down, and into the net flies a shot from Liverpool's Chris Lawler . . .

Old players have told me tales of how they used to look on trips abroad as holidays. They thought they could stay out half the night at parties and still hand out hidings to all and sundry the next day.

It is nothing like that now. From the moment you step on the plane or the boat taking you abroad, right until the final whistle sounds for the end of the last game, there is very little room for relaxation. Everyone is fully committed to the job in hand.

Whenever I feel tension before a game – and the man who says he does not get butterflies in the old 'tum' is a fibber – I find myself thinking of my old Stamford Bridge colleague, Bert Murray, who is now with Birmingham.

It was on my first trip to Australia, when I was just 17. On the way out Bert had kept letting it drop what an expert he was with a boomerang. We had scarcely landed and settled into our hotel when the lads all got together, bought a boomerang and dragged Bert, who had never dreamed he would be put to the test, down to the beach to show his prowess.

We all lined up and Bert, always a trier, took his stance and, winding himself up like a baseball pitcher, let fly.

It was a case of Charlie Drake all over again. Bert's boomerang did not come back! It just flew on and on – never wavering an inch until it flopped into the sea.

'Kick it the next time, Bert. You get more swerve on your in-swinging corner,' was the advice Bert was given.

Daft? Maybe. But it is silly little incidents like this and men like Bert Murray, who can take a joke as well as make one, who do as much as all the meetings to foster team spirit – specially on the long tiresome journeys which are part and parcel of the Soccer scene these days.

❛ **I am not going to say it was a swindle nor a plunder, but it looked like one . . .**

❛ **I dare to say England should not be World Champions . . .**

❛ **On a neutral pitch I am sure the Germans would win five goals to nil . . .** ❜

RATTIN: TWO YEARS AFTER

' The Trophy comes back, in Mexico '

by ANTONIO UBALDO RATTIN

(of Boca Juniors and Argentine)

PEOPLE see me and say: 'We can't believe you were sent off at Wembley when Argentina was defeated by England in the World Cup!'

People believe what they are told or what they think is true. Everybody tells me that in the film 'GOAL!' I can be seen clearly uttering insults. Well, let everyone believe what they want.

The truth is that I shouted insults – of course I did. I sent everyone to hell. *But not the referee.*

Why should I insult the referee? I insulted the F.I.F.A. directive that took me from the field. I insulted it because it exasperated me to see the arbitrary injustice which meant my team was reduced to ten men without any reason.

Such a thing made me lose my self-control! Good gracious . . . ! If England won the World Championship it was because they were host team; because the match was played at Wembley; because everything was prepared to damage the opposition; because it was not fairly played, and everything was arranged beforehand.

I am not going to say it was a swindle or a

Looks like a sitter for Wednesday long-service man John Fantham – he's goalside of Wolves 'keeper Parkes (LEFT, TOP). But Fantham had his shot scrambled off the line! BELOW, another Wednesday striker, John Ritchie, goes on his knees to nod this one through the Wolves defence, but it was wide.

plunder, but it looked like one.

Even further, I dare to say England should not be World Champions.

In my opinion Germany was the best team in the competition. You saw what happened. They were put aside. The Germans were allowed to get to the Final but not to be the Champions, as they deserved.

If those same two teams could play again on a neutral pitch, I am sure the Germans would win by five goals to nil.

be led by statistics, it would not be as interesting or attractive.

When I am asked about the 1966 World Championships I always answer that everything looked prepared beforehand to push the South Americans out. But you can never say what is going to happen or foresee a result.

In Argentina we go on thinking we are the best football players in the world. Facts show us we are

A quieter Rattin – Rattin the family man, with his twin daughters.

I have seen many things in the years I have played football, for I began playing for Boca Juniors in 1956 and was in the Argentine selection three years later. I have a good position in life thanks to football but my gratitude does not make me blind.

In London, England were not the best team, and they became Champions. In 1962 Chile, the hosts, were third. And what afterwards happened to Chile? In 1958 Sweden were host country and runners-up. What afterwards happened to Sweden?

In 1954 the Hungarians were the best. What happened to them? In 1950 the Uruguayans won and astonished the Brazilians who were the favourites till that moment.

Yes, you get many surprises in football. If there were any logic in it, if it were a science, if you could

wrong.

What reason have we to be so proud? Who did we beat to say we are the best? With that way of thinking we'll never be Champions so we must change.

Why can't we be more humble and work with more discipline and less pride? Isn't it truth that we have always needed five cents to get a peso? Of course!

We played in the final of an Olympic Championship and Uruguay defeated us. We played in the finals in the first World Championship and Uruguay also defeated us.

Our neighbours the Uruguayans also say they are the best football players in the world. But they have a reason to say so. They have two Olympic titles,

'Why can't we Argentinians be more humble and work with more discipline and less pride?' asks Rattin. Glasgow Celtic, among others, will agree with that. TOP RIGHT, Celtic men let Racing defender Alfio Basile know what they think of the Argentinian's tough tactics. BELOW, the golden head of skipper Billy McNeill scores a winner against Racing at Parkhead.

two World Championships, three Trophies of America, two Inter-continental Trophies. And what have we got?

With the strange things that happen I was suspended for five games to justify those persons from the F.I.F.A. One of these days we will train a team of eleven masons and become World Champions.

I have been asked if England might be Champions in Mexico. I don't think they will be. They can't be.

I am deeply convinced that to win in 1966 England needed to play at Wembley. In 1970 in Mexico they won't be able to win, don't let them even dream of winning!

World Championships are a declared war of blood and fire. Americans were put aside in Europe. Do you think that European teams are going to be any luckier in Mexico?

In 1970 the Trophy comes back to our Continent.

There is no doubt that in 1966 things were not right. There were stratagems and tricks of all kinds in order to damage us. I hope those things won't happen again for the sake of the sport.

Let us go on talking about football. That football which makes crowds passionate, but which runs the risk of dying one of these days.

A possible improvement in the off-side rule is already being considered – but shall we get it? There are elements in favour and against. Have they been well considered? And won't it be just the same even if we change it? Won't the watch on the attackers increase? Won't play be from area to area leaving the middle field to itself?

I don't even want to consider that fact. Nevertheless, a match that finishes nine goals to eight is much more agreeable to watch than one that finishes one to nil. But, although I seem a passionate and an emotional person, I think things must be well thought out before changes are made.

Every morning, on the 40-minute drive from my home to Boca's training, I think about football. What it has given me; what it has furnished me; and the experience. I leave my four-year-old twins playing, and drive fast, thinking what football means to me.

But I get exasperated when I think about Wembley, the plunder of the match, won by one to nil by England.

I think about the officials who tried to take me from the field, the fans whistling, and my companions dominated by amazement and anger, realising that the Argentine's effort of months and months was lost due to an injustice.

We were South Americans, that explained everything. Because South Americans were an obstacle in England's way to the Trophy.

That is why I think they won't be Champions. The 1970 World Championship won't be at Wembley . . .!

Celtic goal-grabber Willie Wallace (LEFT) almost snatches an early lead for Celtic, but Racing 'keeper Cejas punches the ball away from his head. BELOW, Cejas does it again! – Bobby Lennox (far right) stabs the ball goalwards at virtually point-blank range but Cejas smothers the effort courageously.

● The International Football Book is ten years old with this issue.

SOCCER'S COMMON

● Through the years Matt Busby, a regular and valued contributor, has been staunchly in favour of a steady extension of international contact and competition.

MARKET ALSO HAS

● But now Mr. Busby—first-ever winner of the International Football Book's Football Sword of Honour—enters a note of caution.

ITS BIG SNAGS

● 'Let us make haste slowly' he says, 'and iron out a few more of the problems before we rush into a European Super-League'.

by MATT BUSBY, C.B.E.
(Manager of Manchester United)

MATT BUSBY

MANCHESTER UNITED have completed another season in Europe, our fourth in the European Cup. Over the last eleven years it was our sixth run in one or other of the major international competitions.

I think Old Trafford can justly claim to have given Manchester in particular and England in general a fair glimpse of foreign football, with all the thrills, anxieties, satisfactions, conflicts and disappointments involved.

Indeed, with the growth in stature of the European Cup Winners' Cup and the Inter Cities' Fairs Cup, qualification for the latter also now depending upon achievement in domestic competition, there has been a sustained supply of European football

'I hope English teams will prosper in the various Continental tournaments, not least Manchester United' – Showing the verve which consistently keeps United top of the popularity chart are George Best (right) and Pat Crerand; Arsenal's Frank McLintock, centre, probably feels like a sparrow swooped on by hawks . . .

up and down the country for the last year or two.

And of course British football has been making a bigger and bigger mark against the Continentals. At national level, our England team in the 1966 World Cup made everyone realise that the balance of Soccer power had swung our way.

Glasgow Celtic emphasised the worthiness of the British style, and the top-class players involved, by winning the European Cup in 1967. I have been increasingly pleased with Manchester United's record in European football.

We have lost vital matches at times, of course, but we have also scored, I think, some impressive results and only rarely have we really let ourselves down.

Yet despite this impressive march into Europe by British football, what has happened to the demand for some kind of Continental Super League, with our clubs taking part?

Not so long ago it was all the rage to urge a permanent European Championship with one or two clubs from eight or nine countries competing in a League.

It was fashionable to claim that this was the future for football, with jet air travel making it all possible.

Now we don't hear so much of this kind of talk – and a good thing too! But let me make my position clear. I am a confirmed believer in venturing into Europe and I think Manchester United's record in this respect supports this attitude.

English football remained too insular for too long and – we know only too well – we got left behind.

But I think the clamour for a Super League a few years ago was a hysterical reaction, a tendency to under-sell British football and think that everything good comes from across the Channel.

Now I hope we know better and last season showed us a few of the snags that would be accentuated if we played regularly in a European Super League.

Liverpool's Bill Shankly, who criticised the Italian referee after their game against Hungary's Ferenc-

More of that crowd-pulling United action: and it's young Brian Kidd, centre, pressing Arsenal 'keeper Jim Furnell. But the ball goes to Ian Ure (No. 6) and he clears . . .

aros in Budapest, said there was the constant worry f what was going to happen next, the different nterpretation of this and that, and the constant anger of flare-ups through provocative opponents.

Maybe Shankly was unusually depressed at the me, but he certainly shocked many advocates of a uper League when he said: 'I do not think a educed Football League programme is the answer.

wouldn't like to think that a British city would ose their club because of our consideration of uropean Soccer.

'*The idea of a European Super League is too full of roblems.*'

After coming back from France, where his Spurs layed Lyons, manager Bill Nicholson put his finger n the two big obstacles that hold up ideas of a uper League with the Continent.

'We do not speak the same language. It is impos-ible for a Czech referee to control English and rench players when nobody is really aware of vhat the referee is trying to achieve.

Manchester City's Doyle, BELOW, looks as if he's about to lay out United eeper Alec Stepney with one of those 'tele-wrestling' holds! But all was ell. Not so, RIGHT, with United's giant, Denis Law – caught, eyes rned heavenward, a few seconds after missing a penalty against Coventry City . . .

'While the Continental referees ignore fouls like pulling and handing off, they immediately penalise perfectly fair tackles and charges.

'*The Continentals are encouraged to fly off the handle at any firm tackle and that is how the rows start.*'

The Spurs chief had every reason to feel angry. He had three players injured, one needing ten stitches to a leg wound, another kicked in the mouth and the third punched in the face.

There are critics of football who blame everything on the players' temperament or money, and excuse the referee, saying that he doesn't start the rough stuff. It is easy to dismiss the problem this way, but to do so ignores the facts.

There are cheats in every sport and it is not confined to professionalism. Amateur footballers and even Rugby Union types are not above giving vent to their feelings when they feel aggrieved, or committing unfair acts during the game.

Take a look at the lists of 'crimes' in amateur Soccer and Rugby Union and you will find proof that money is not always the root of evil.

When the game is played with opponents who seem to interpret the rules differently and get away with things we would call fouls, is it any wonder that the flame is lit for an explosion?

These then are the problems. We mustn't run away from them. As a pioneer of entering the European Common Market in Soccer, I hope we shall all grow closer in our interpretation of the game and I hope English teams will prosper in the various Continental tournaments, not least Manchester United.

But as I look to the future of football I am proud of the British contribution, its standards and the skill of our players. It adds up to a top-class League Championship competition and an exciting F.A. Cup tournament.

Let us foray into Europe by all means, but let us make haste slowly and iron out a few more of the problems before we rush into a Super League.

'*When the game is played with opponents who seem to interpret the rules differently . . . is it any wonder that the flame is lit for an explosion?*' – LEFT, ABOVE, *Celtic's Willie Wallace gives Dukla 'keeper Ivo Viktor no chance with this first of his two goals. But* BELOW, *trouble!* – *Dukla wing-half Gelega rolls in agony after being tackled by Steve Chalmers . . . and the Czechs swarm angrily.* RIGHT, *the nervous toll of a top game – as seen in the face of United star Bobby Charlton.*

TONY HATELEY

THE KOP, THE DOC, AND ME!

HAVE you ever tried to imagine that you are a footballer – a footballer for whom some top-class club has just forked out £100,000 If you haven't, just put yourself in my boots . . and try to work out how you would feel.

I've travelled a fair way in football, in a comparatively short time: Notts County to Aston Villa . . Villa to Chelsea . . . Chelsea to Liverpool. And in the process, I've clocked up a pretty hefty record of transfer fees. Considerably more than £200,000 changed hands, in total, during my travels from the Midlands to London, and then to Merseyside

When you stop to think about it, this is enough to give *anyone* the shivers. While it might make you smile to think that, once upon a time, Sunderland transferred a player called Alf Common to Middlesbrough for the sum of £1,000, the fact remains that almost certainly Alf and I had *something* in common And no pun intended . . .

by TONY HATELEY
(Liverpool's £100,000 forward)

That £1,000 fee was the first any club had ever splashed out on a player. The date was February 1905. Now, of course, I never even saw Alf Common play. But I'm willing to take a bet that when he made his début for Middlesbrough, he felt just the same as I did . . . somewhat nervous.

Only I've had that feeling two or three times, now.

There *are* a few players who never seem to suffer from nerves. I wish I could say I was one. But that wouldn't be 100 per cent true.

I know only a handful of footballers who don't worry, when something big is at stake – like an international match, or their League début – even if they haven't been transferred for money. But when you have a £100,000 tag hung around your neck, well . . . it wouldn't be human to go out with a gay smile and not a care in the world.

They say that I didn't settle in at Chelsea; they say that Chelsea's style wasn't my style at all; they say a lot of things . . . and I suppose that, to some extent, many things came into it, when you consider whether or not Chelsea got value for money

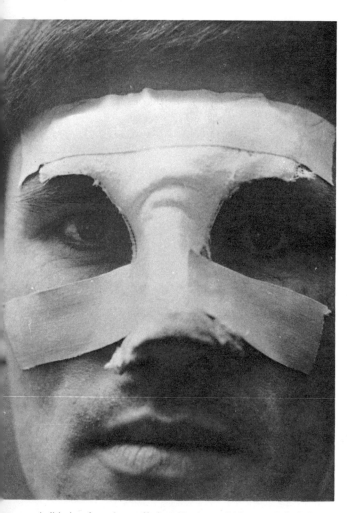

Auditioning for a horror film? – No, just a fairly normal football accident: Tony Hateley, a day or two after breaking his nose . . .

Money meets money – High-priced Tony Hateley clashes with high-priced Mike England, the Spurs and Wales centre-half.

All I know is that I did my best for Chelsea – and I have one fabulous memory of my days at Stamford Bridge, even now. I scored the goal that took Chelsea to Wembley in the F.A. Cup. That was the day that Tommy Docherty said: 'It was the £100,000 goal . . . that's what I bought him for.'

Since that day, things have changed both for myself and 'The Doc'. Tommy made his exit from Stamford Bridge, and took on the job of trying to put Rotherham back on their Second Division feet. I'll say this for Tommy – he has courage. The courage of his convictions.

But what about me? I confess I got the shock of my life when I was told Liverpool manager Bill Shankly was wanting to sign me. Frankly, I wondered if any club again would venture to splash such a large sum of money on me. But Liverpool's offer fell only £5,000 short of the figure Chelsea had paid for my services.

Bill Shankly is a canny Scot – and a Soccer fanatic. Which is one reason I decided that Liverpool could be the right club for me. Our manager doesn't waste two words, if one will do. But get him on Soccer, and he'll talk all day and night! Good sense, too.

It's well known that Bill Shankly is a fitness fanatic, as well as a football fanatic. He was a great player, and he's been a great manager. With the staff he has built up backstage at Anfield, any player joining Liverpool will become better.

For a start, his fitness will improve – no matter *how* fit he thought he was when he arrived. For another thing, his ability will improve – no matter *how* good he was when he arrived.

But I think that one of the secrets of Bill Shankly's success has not been noted as it should. For above all, I rate the Liverpool manager as a real psychologist. If you didn't particularly believe in yourself when you joined Liverpool, you'll think you're great after half an hour's spiel from 'the boss'.

And if, with all due modesty, you thought you were the best player in the country when you joined, that 30-minute pep-talk will convince you that you were being *too* modest: you're the greatest player in the world!

There was one famous manager about whom they used to joke. They said that his trouble was

'With the service Roger Hunt and I got from Ian St. John . . . some teams were going to suffer!' – LEFT, *bared teeth emphasise some of that famous St. John determination.* RIGHT, TOP, *a winner for Tommy Smith – his penalty kick spins through the hands of Stoke and England 'keeper Gordon Banks;* BELOW, *not so good for Smith! – Spurs' young Dennis Bond, left, wrong-foots him.*

he believed there had only ever been one great player – himself. So his men tended to get an inferiority complex.

Bill Shankly *was* a great player – but he never tells you he was. What he does tell you is what a fine player *you* are . . . and what a great *team* the lot of you make, together.

I knew, when I signed for Liverpool, that 'the boss' was buying my goal-scoring services. I'm big, I'm rated as being especially good in the air, I'm a centre-forward . . . and so it's my job to score goals.

I also knew that I would have to contend with two things – the Kop, and Roger Hunt's popularity. 'The boss' recognised these things, too. And the way he saw it, Roger and I should be good for each other – and the Kop should be good for us both.

Instead of one big fellow up front, Liverpool would have a twin partnership – and with the service Roger and I got from Ian St. John and wingers Peter Thompson and Ian Callaghan, some teams were going to suffer!

Well, I said at the start that I wouldn't have been human, if I hadn't wondered a bit about the Kop and the price tag round my neck. But when you start scoring goals, the Kop makes you want to score more – and when you go off the goal standard for a spell, there's 'Doctor' Bill Shankly always ready with a verbal pick-me-up!

It stands to reason that there must be *some* players in Britain who are at least as good as the Anfield brigade. But you don't even *think* such things, when 'Doctor' Shankly is about! After playing for one 'Doc' at Stamford Bridge, now I'm playing for another . . .

I've called 'the boss' a psychologist . . . and I suppose he really is. But there's one other thing. He's an honest man. With him, there is neither time nor room for humbug. So it just occurs to me that when he tells us we're the greatest, he really believes that we *are* the greatest. And maybe that's why we *do* win so many matches.

They say that home is where the heart is – and Bill Shankly's heart is with Liverpool. He believes in every single one of his players, from the first team to the juniors. And when you've got a boss like that, you just can't let him down. Liverpool? – They're the greatest!

The crunch! – in close-up. It's white-shirted David Sadler of Manchester United having his shot blocked by Liverpool 'keeper Tommy Lawrence with Ron Yeats heaving up in support.

TOP TWENTY

more sketches of top world stars by **BRIAN GLANVILLE**

Bertie Auld . . . rich dividends.

BERTIE AULD (Celtic and Scotland). Now in his second spell with Celtic; transformed from a moderate outside-left to an outstanding midfield player; one of the chief inspirations of Celtic's victory in the 1967 European Cup. Born in Glasgow, small but solidly built, Auld grew up with Celtic, was capped in 1959 for Scotland against Wales, went to Birmingham City and there scored a good many goals, but did not develop as a footballer. He rejoined his old club just before Jock Stein took over as manager, and was transformed into a linking player. As such, his energy, ball control and swift, accurate passing has paid rich dividends, winning him, and the club, honours in League, Cup, League Cup and European Cup.

Alfio Basile (Racing Club). Born at Bahia Blanca, November 1, 1943; a tall, powerful, sometimes over-robust player, he was one of those sent off the field, like Auld (who wouldn't go!), in the notorious Racing v. Celtic match in Montevideo. Since Racing won it, however, he has added a world club's title to those he had won with Racing in the Argentinian Championship (which included a 39-match unbeaten run) and the South American Cup of 1967. A versatile footballer who plays as a stopper left-half, he is also adept at counter-attacking, and he has a powerful left-foot shot.

Paolo Borges (Bangu and Brazil). Did not quite contrive to get into Brazil's World Cup team, though many thought he should have been chosen. A winger of pace, astonishing ball control and the ability to score goals. The Brazilians recalled him from Houston, where he was playing for Bangu, to play in their three-match series against Uruguay in Montevideo during the summer of 1967. Previously,

he'd helped his club to win the Championship of Rio. A major Brazilian hope for the 1970 World Cup, he is still in his early twenties. He has the almost impertinent 'fantasy' of the finest Brazilian players, and has added subtlety and judgement to his great natural gifts.

Anatoli Bychevetz (Kiev Dynamo and Russia). It was lucky for Russia and for Kiev that the World Cup indirectly gave this fine young winger his chance. So many players were called up from Kiev for World Cup training that they had to put in reserves. So Bychevetz emerged as a brave, strong, fast, aggressive striker. In 1967, at 21, he proved

59

himself the hammer of the Scots, unsettling their defence when Russia beat them at Hampden, then going on to score vital goals against Celtic in the first round of the European Cup. An immensely talented player technically and tactically, he may yet prove the best winger Russia has produced.

Johan Cruyff (Ajax and Holland). A young centre-forward of immense potential and exceptional finishing power, Cruyff fully established himself during season 1966–67, when he was one of the chief reasons for Ajax Amsterdam's run in the European Cup; Liverpool in particular could do nothing with him. A moment of anger when playing for Holland against Czechoslovakia – he allegedly struck the referee – led to his own Federation suspending him from international football for almost a year. He came into the Ajax side as a young reserve – 20 years old – in season 1965–66, scored a couple of goals and stayed. Has great acceleration and initiative, together with a powerful shot, and skilled control.

Robert Herbin (St. Étienne and France). An immensely versatile footballer who can play as a link man – perhaps his best position – a striker or even a centre-half, the red-haired Herbin did remarkably well against England in the 1966 World Cup, though severely injured. Born in Paris, March 3, 1939, Herbin actually was launched by Cavigal of Nice, where his mentor was a M. Rémond. Excellent in the air, he made his name as a defender winning the first of his many caps for France as centre-half against Yugoslavia in Paris in July, 1960 – a European Nations Cup semi-final which France lost 5–4. Then he had to wait till April, 1962, for a second cap, at right-half against Poland, France losing in Paris once again. His favourite position, however, has always been in attack.

Pedro Eugenio De Felipe (Real Madrid and Spain). A powerful centre-half who was born in Madrid, February 2, 1944, came up through the Real junior teams, and modelled himself – as one can easily see – on their rugged Uruguayan centre-

...alf, Santamaria. De Felipe himself has said that those who see him in action on the field may be surprised to hear he has so mild a character off it. ...ucceeded his hero in the Real defence, winning ...panish Championship medals, and of course a ...uropean Cup Final medal in 1966, when Real ...efeated Partizan. Capped for Spain the following ...eason, he was unlucky to be injured playing for ...hem against the Rest of the World in Ricardo ...amora's jubilee match in September, 1967, drop-...ing out for a number of weeks. But, at 22, it was ...lear enough much more would be heard from him.

Mike England (Tottenham Hotspur and Wales). ...entre-half, born at Holywell, discovered and ...eveloped by Blackburn Rovers. While at Ewood ...ark, he solidly established himself in the Welsh ...nternational team, where he has been a fitting ...uccessor to Ray Daniel and the Charles brothers. ...lmost unbeatable in the air, he is also mobile and ...trong on the ground. He specialises in coming up ...or corner kicks, and has headed many a good goal. ...fter a long dispute with Blackburn, he at last ...btained a transfer in 1966, joining Spurs for £95,000. At the end of his first season at Tottenham, ...e won a Cup Final medal against Chelsea. He was ...hen still only 24.

Jimmy Johnstone (Celtic and Scotland). A ...ittle, stocky, red-haired outside-right who won ...more admiration than any Celtic player on their ...ath to the European Cup; and more vicious ...uffeting than any other, when they played Racing ...n the world final. A superb ball player with fine ...cceleration, great courage and a powerful right-...ooted shot, Johnstone is the living refutation of the ...heory that the orthodox winger is dead. Two fine ...oals against England at Hampden in 1966 estab-...ished him as an international. Often in the wars, ...requently provoked, Johnstone was sent off during ...he world club play-off in Montevideo; finally ...exasperated after continually brutal treatment. A ...Celtic product.

Dirceu Lopes (Cruzeiro and Brazil). An inside-...eft who was only 20 years old when he played a ...major part in his team's elimination of Santos from ...the 1967 Brazilian Cup. Till then, Cruzeiro, from ...Belo Horizonte, had been merely an unfashionable ...provincial club. Lopes is an excellent ball player, very fast and inventive, who plays in midfield but can also go forward to score goals. He won his first Brazilian cap against Uruguay in the summer of 1967, when Brazil went to Montevideo to play their three-match series. Should certainly figure in their 1970 World Cup team. Nicknamed 'The Little Prince', he has a fine swerve and a deadly left foot.

Roger Magnusson (Juventus and Sweden). Spent the 1967–68 season in the ridiculous situation of a reserve de luxe, unable to play for Juventus in the Italian Championship, but kept on ice, with special permission, to figure in European Cup matches when wanted. The previous season he'd been lent to Cologne. Tall and strong, he is an outside-right with a wonderful swerve and a fine burst of speed, who moves far more gracefully than his rather ungainly build suggests. He developed with A.I.K. and so won the admiration of the Brazilians that Flamengo invited him to spend some weeks with them in Rio.

Rachid Mekloufi (St. Étienne, France and Morocco). Born at Setif, August 12, 1936, an inside-right or centre-forward of considerable gifts. Would have played many more times for France had he not, during the North African crisis, gone home to play for his own country. But after it was over, he returned – no longer eligible for France, but able to inspire St. Étienne in the Championship, in 1966–67. A shrewd, constructive footballer with clever control, he was first capped for France as a 20-year-old against Russia, whom they beat 2–1 in Paris on October 21, 1956. One of the eight children of a police inspector, he was encouraged as a child by British soldiers, who paid him five francs a goal!

Kalman Meszoly (Vasas and Hungary). An outstanding player in the 1962 World Cup, a still

iner one in 1966, when he was transformed from a topper centre-half into a splendid all-purpose foot-baller, often surging into attack. Tall, blond and well-built, Meszoly was a great success in Chile, where he was particularly admired during the World Cup by the England players. Born July 13, 1941.

Terry Neill (Arsenal and Ireland). Came to Arsenal as a teenaged right-half, from Bangor City, but it was Ireland who, when he was only 18, successfully transformed him into a centre-half for their European tour of 1961. Since then he has developed into a forceful and accomplished stopper for both club and country, solid on the field, lively and intelligent off it. Excellent in the air, and a formidable tackler. Born Belfast.

Ermindo Onega (River Plate and Argentina). One of the cleverest ball-playing inside-forwards of the 1966 World Cup, Onega moves beautifully and passes with great skill and cunning. His partnership with Artime, built up at River Plate before Artime went to Independiente, was particularly impressive that July. Curiously, both players had a chequered career with River, frequently being left out of the side. They even played for Argentina against Paraguay in the World Cup qualifiers while in River Plate reserves, an experience which befell

Onega again after the 1966 World Cup. Born in 1941 in the province of Santa Fé, he joined River as a 17-year-old and was in the first team within six months. He can also play on the right wing and had a brother, Daniel, with him at River. Criticised at times for alleged lack of combativity, his technique is outside discussion.

Roberto Perfumo (Racing Club and Argentina). An elegant defender, still in his early twenties; poised, intelligent and technically adroit, specialising in the scissor-kick overhead clearance. Nominally right-back though he actually plays either as second centre-half or, if necessary, as sweeper. A successful member of the 1966 Argentina World Cup side in England, he also looked impressively cool and resourceful as the key man of Racing's defence at Hampden, in the world club final against Celtic of 1967. A Racing development; played in the 1964 Olympic team.

Luigi Riva (Cagliari and Italy). Came back strongly and bravely in 1967 from a leg broken while under full sail in the Italian Championship. Indeed, his 18 goals still left him top scorer when it was over. Born at Leggiuno (Varese), in the North, on November 7, 1944, he began in Series C (3rd Division) with Legnano in 1962–63, played for Italy in the 1963 European Youth Tournament in England, joined Cagliari the following season. An

immy Johnstone (left) . . . scoring for Celtic against another 'Top Twenty' star, Ivo Viktor of Dukla.

outside-left of speed and incision, he won his first
cap away to Hungary in June, 1965, another against
France in Paris the following year, but didn't get
into the World Cup twenty-two. Returned to the
national side against Cyprus in November, 1967 –
with three goals.

Josip Skoblar (Hanover and Yugoslavia). Born
in 1941, he made his name and won more than
twenty Yugoslav caps as an outside-left with O.F.K.
Belgrade; fast, elusive and a very frequent scorer.
In 1966 he was transferred to Hanover who, unable
to use him that season, lent him to Marseilles,
where he played brilliantly, mostly at inside-left.
Joining Hanover for the 1967–68 season, he almost
at once was sent off the field and given a long sus-
pension, though the Germans generously allowed
him to play for Yugoslavia against them in the
Nations Cup.

Edouard Streltsov (Torpedo and Russia). Has
had an extraordinary career indeed. Emerged in
the '50s as an excellent centre-forward, winning
caps for Russia, and considered one of their strong
points for the 1958 World Cup. Shortly before it
took place, however, he was accused of assault on a
girl, found guilty and sent for twelve years to a
labour camp. Amnestied in 1965, he was at first
allowed to play for his club only in Russia. But at

the beginning of season 1966–67 he returned at last
to the full national team, leading the attack in
Milan against Italy. Sad indeed that so fine a
player should have been obliged to miss three
World Cups; though he will doubtless have some
consolation in his membership of the 1970 team.

Ivo Viktor (Dukla Prague and Czechoslovakia).
One of the best goalkeepers to emerge for many
years, he played superbly against England at
Wembley in 1966, when the Czechs held them to
a 0–0 draw at Wembley; and Viktor held everything in sight. His calmness that evening, his
masterly fielding of the high cross, stamped him
as a player with a splendid future. Born in Brno,
where he learned his football, he is one of the many
players who came to Dukla during army service.
First capped in 1966 against Brazil.

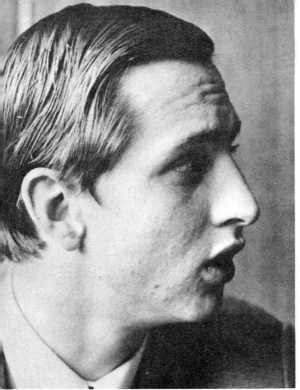

JOHAN CRUYFF

Too-Strict Discipline in England

by JOHAN CRUYFF

(Centre-forward of Ajax Amsterdam and Holland)

IT seems as far away as ever, but the game as a whole needs a European League more urgently with every season that passes. Money is becoming more and more important and there are very few countries who can really afford to plod along with their own domestic Championship.

The biggest single argument in favour of the European League is the clear fact that there simply are not enough top-class players to go round. With anything from sixteen to twenty-two clubs in the top class it means that talent is too thinly spread to maintain a consistently high standard of play all round.

Here in Holland, for example, there are only two

'Cruyffie' – as seen by Dik, Holland's sports cartoonist.

or three clubs who can even dream of matching the big clubs, Fejenoord of Rotterdam and my own club Ajax. Perhaps four or five times a season we really have to struggle to win, but the rest of the season results are almost a foregone conclusion.

Perhaps I should say *were* a foregone conclusion – for in the last year or two it seems that everyone has decided to play defensively. Though the result is the same – a win for Ajax or Fejenoord – the winning margin is trimmed from five or six goals to only one or two, but the result is the same in terms of League points.

For the fans, however, it's another matter

altogether, for it cannot be interesting to watch match in which one team commits itself almo wholly to defence.

Against Fejenoord, the team with the ball attack and moments later when they've lost the ball, the have to defend. The game flows from end to end It's thrilling to watch, interesting and exhilaratin to play in. This is the kind of football the publi should be offered every week, but we'll never b able to do it if we stick to our traditional nationa Championships.

In Holland only 85 players in the whole country ear more than £1,000 a year from football, and a good mar of them are with Ajax and Fejenoord.

The rest have to supplement their income wit another job outside the game, and that's an awfu lot of players when you realise that we have 57 pro fessional clubs. Only ten of the 57 have an averag gate of 10,000 a game and for many clubs the figur is around 3,000. If the standards are going to ris then the players have to be paid. There's no escap from this viewpoint. It means attractive matche every week to pull in the crowds.

Although the professional aspect is emphasise this can be overdone. My feeling is that man people think we players think about nothing bu money. It just isn't so.

Walking off the ground after being beaten I fee only disappointment, and I'm sure the majority o professional players feel the same way. I've neve heard money mentioned on the pitch or in th dressing room at any time, and never thought abou it either.

Perhaps it's different in other countries, though shouldn't think so. Certainly there are difference in approach and in training for example and thi helps increase the appeal of a European League Meeting foreign teams every week would increas the enthusiasm of everyone concerned, for there' a great deal to be learned about this game.

Although I wouldn't regard myself as an authorit I would say without much doubt that Dutch player are more intelligent and more flexible than thei English counterparts. My experience of playin

'Everyone has decided to play defensively,' says Cruyff – but not always one hopes, with the help of an arm-lock, as suffered here by Cruyff himself FACING PAGE, *a flash . . . almost a shadow . . . but to Liverpool goal keeper Tommy Lawrence the presence of dashing Johan Cruyff seems ver real indeed . . .*

against English, German and Italian players is that players in these countries are under the very strict control of their managers.

I played for Ajax against Liverpool, for example, in the European Cup and was amazed to find that I was free to move around without being marked. It seemed to me that the Liverpool manager had told his players how they were to play. After the interval it was quite different and for the rest of the game I had a man tight on me. Discipline is too strict in England, Germany and Italy, and the players don't make changes unless the manager orders it.

At Ajax it's quite different. If we find that we cannot make progress down the middle then we play on the wings, and if we find that defenders are better in the air than we are then we change and play the ball low. It must be a question of training methods, I think.

With Ajax we spend a lot of our training time in possession games. Three against two and 'one touch', for example, and this builds up our independence and individuality. We haven't run round the ground in training for more than three years!

If I have to describe my attitude to the game I would say that I am half sportsman and half artist, but bearing in mind that my playing career will be short I have to be something of a businessman, too. In this sense I think the English have a better understanding of professional players than do the Dutch.

In particular this applies to referees and officials and perhaps it is understandable for in Holland we have only been professionals since 1954.

This opinion is based on my personal experience two years ago when I was sent off in an international match. At the time, spectators thought I had been sent off for kicking an opponent, but I honestly had no idea why I was ordered off.

In his report the referee said: 'Cruyff hit me.'

I couldn't believe it and at the F.A. hearing I protested my innocence. T.V. provided a film of the match and the Disciplinary Committee ran this film through seven times before they were satisfied. Finally they said: 'We cannot say that you did hit the referee but we have decided that you were unsporting.'

I was banned from playing in the national team for one year. Can you imagine how that made me feel?

GEORGE BEST says—

'Don't worry!—I'll never trip over my wallet'

by GEORGE BEST
(Manchester United and Northern Ireland)

I WAS in the middle of what the sports-writers call a 'mazy dribble'. A League match in which Manchester United were already three up, and I felt I could take a few chances. So I waltzed round a couple of defenders then took on one more.

There was this yell: 'Don't worry about Bestie – he'll soon trip over his wallet!'

So happens I didn't. But this raucous yell underlined one of the worries about being in top-class football today. Some fans resent a player having any outside-the-game interests. They seem to think that when a footballer starts earning big money as a star . . . that that's the only thing in his life.

Well, I happen to think that money should be used to make more money and most certainly I think that a footballer should have interests *outside* the game.

I won't ever trip over my wallet whether things are going well or super well. To me, football is my great ambition – and by that I mean I hope that I'll never stop learning and will always be able to add some improvement to my game.

Unfortunately I've this name of being both a party-lover *and* a business man who is interested in getting enough money together to retire. Well, all right. I *do* like going to parties and I like meeting pretty girls. But I'd never stay out too late, or drink too much, or do anything else that would prevent me from turning in a Soccer performance that was as good as possible.

I want to earn money, from outside business interests, simply because I know what it's like to be poor – and because I don't see why footballers should be regarded as morons.

I don't see any reason why a professional footballer, in these days, shouldn't be a businessman as well as a star player. If a professional singer, or comedian

Minutes to go to kick-off in the Ireland v. Scotland international, but for two young men of the world the rule is cool detachment and a friendly word – even though, on the day, Manchester United club-mates George Best and Denis Law are in opposing teams . . .

For his parents, Ann and Richard Best, George bought this fish restaurant . . . on a flying visit he helps out!

becomes owner of a block of flats, and earns money from it, then nobody feels that he is liable to put on a bad performance because he's involved elsewhere.

Take a look at the pictures of the old-time football teams. I mean no disrespect, but the fact is that they don't even *look* as if they have outside interests! There was a maximum wage then, of about twenty quid a week, but even so it was good money and a footballer tended to stay in the one business.

I was dead lucky. When I came into the game, there was no maximum wage and so, if I was good enough, I would get the sort of money that proved I was worth being in the top bracket. I knew all about boxers and the way they earned big money and still managed to end with nothing more than a very hard glare from their bank managers.

I wanted to make my money *earn* money. I had to make a choice on the type of business. I knew little about some things; less than nothing about most. But I'd always been clothes-conscious. When I first signed professional forms with Manchester United, I often spent £35 a week on shirts and suits and way-out gear.

Now I was a pretty normal sort of bloke, even if I had more money than most at that age, so I started studying the boutique business. I even designed a special type of trousers which sold well once I'd got my own boutique.

The trouble is that it tended to set a precedent. Everybody started writing about me being a boutique-owner and making that more important than the fact that I played for Manchester United. Suddenly the money bit became vital. 'George Best wants to make money so he can retire early and lounge around' . . . well, nobody actually wrote that, but you could read between the lines.

Fact is, I'm only twenty-two now and I think I'm learning enough about football to be able to go on for years and years, keeping myself out of trouble and avoiding burning myself out. Maybe not as long as Stanley Matthews, whom I idolised, but for many years yet. And football will always be the most important thing to me. It's the life I've wanted since I was just a wee kid back home in Belfast. . . .

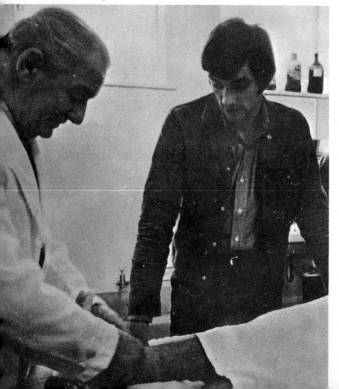

'They forgot about the training and the time spent on a cold cot in the trainer's department . . .' – George Best watches United physiotherapist Ted Dalton at work. FACING PAGE, *United don't always have it their own way, as witness the dismay of Stepney and Burns as Southampton's Ron Davies scores a good 'un at Old Trafford.*

But I also recall the old arguments about me being a professional footballer. People reckoned it wasn't even a full-time job. Getting paid all that money for working just ninety minutes a week – that's what they said. They forgot about the training and the time spent on a cold cot in the trainer's department.

But it was true, in a sense. We *did* have a lot of spare-time. So some footballers tended to go off and follow the gee-gees, others hung around in billiard-rooms and others just hung around with those that hung around.

I didn't want that. I wanted to enjoy life but I also wanted to build up something that would give me security. I regard my business interests as being a form of relaxation. If I'm dabbling with shirts and shorts, then I'm not allowing myself to get worried about the football scene. Which means that I go into Saturday's game with an easier mind than some of my team-mates.

The difficulty comes when I happen to have a bad game. Then all the old arguments are trotted out. Old party-goer Best is slipping because he spends his time thinking about the girl-friends, or

Football's wisest man – and the two most important women in his life! Matt Busby, wearing the collar of the C.B.E., receives the freedom of the City of Manchester in the company of his mother, Mrs. Helen Busby (left), and his wife, Jean.

Manchester United – and that special 'snap' they reserve for Europe,
LEFT, TOP, *it's Aston left-footing United's first against Sarajevo, in the*
European Cup; BELOW, *it's David Sadler – with a fine header that just*
scraped over . . .

he boutique, or his professional writing jobs. It's
more difficult for me to have a bad patch than
most players.

And the fact that I'm getting much more responsible in outlook nowadays passes unnoticed.

I can't see people feeling sorry for me over all this but I
do just want to underline the fact that I've become a marked
man in more senses than one!

I believe it's time that more footballers took a
serious look at the future and added extra means of
income. The shortest career I know is that of a
professional footballer. Which is why I'm so posi-
tive that having a career in business as well as in
football *does* mix . . . and mix well, just so long as
you don't let the outside career run away with you.

Mark you, I've been lucky. If I'd been taken
with collecting stamps, I'd never have made money
out of this 'hobby'. But men's fashions have always
been an interest – and so have other things for
young people, like Pop records and magazines and
discotheques. Therefore I've been able to use what
money I can spare to build up something worth
while.

But basically I remain a thoroughly dedicated
footballer. If someone came along and forced me
to make a choice between Soccer with Manchester
United and being Charles Clore . . . well, I'd take
Soccer every time. Mind you, I'd reserve the right
to chase after Charles Clore once my playing days
were over!

A luckier header for Sadler, BELOW – *Though surrounded by seven Everton men he's nodding home a goal for United.*

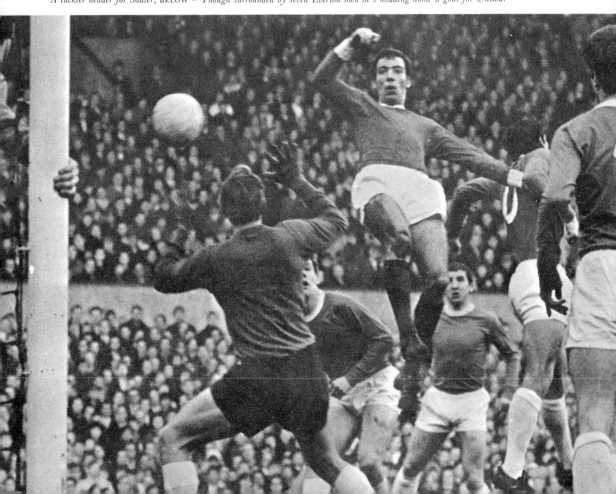

GOLDEN BOY?—MORE A GOLDEN SLAVE!

—says Germany's first player millionaire, HELMUT HALLER

by HELMUT HALLER
(Bologna and West Germany)

THERE are still slaves for sale in Europe today. Very modern slaves, though. Well-fed, well-clad, well-paid.

I know but too well, since I am one of them myself: Helmut Haller, 29 years old, and Germany's first Soccer millionaire.

Yes, sir – I've got my pockets full with all the money I could dream of. But I am no more free than any slave in ancient Rome. Why? I am playing professional Soccer in Italy. This country can be Heaven and Hell for any player – both at the same time.

Italy, that's how they call the golden cage in which they are keeping me. Nowhere else can you make as much money and get wrapped in luxury

It's been a secret so far . . . I pinched the ball with which we played he Wembley World Cup Final' – ABOVE, Helmut Haller in action in he Final against Nobby Stiles, Geoff Hurst and Bobby Charlton. And IGHT, the end of the match – and the last any Englishman saw of Haller's prize souvenir; the match ball!

'I PINCHED THE BALL
FROM WEMBLEY FINAL'

by simply playing football. But nowhere else, mind you, are contracts as tight.

When I left my home club, B.C. Augsburg, seven years ago, I thought that all my problems had been solved for the rest of my life. I had signed a contract binding me to famous F.C. Bologna for better or worse.

Ever since, I have been the Club's personal property, and will remain so even after my present contract has expired. In theory, Bologna's President could, at his discretion, sell me to any other club in the world. As I said before: I am their slave, and they can dispose of me the way they please.

There is just one little 'extra' I managed to squeeze out of them when signing the dotted line: they have to ask for my consent to the new club to which they sell me.

Believe me, it has been a strain to obey the strict rules laid down in my contract. More than once i these years trouble was heading my way.

Years ago, I wanted to return to Germany fo personal reasons. The bosses of Bologna put in the veto. They talked to me for hours on end. And if comes to talking, you can't beat an Italian. S finally I threw in the towel.

Later, famous clubs like Inter.-Milan, F.C Zurich and F.C. Napoli came forth with far bett financial offers. I would gladly have said Yes. Bu I had to say No.

Helmut Haller did not belong to Helmut Halle He belonged to his club. Exclusively.

A few years ago, I really got angry. It happene when my little daughter Karin and her broth Jürgen reached school age. My wife wanted the to attend a German school. There was none Bologna. There seemed to be but one way ou

My streak of bad luck had come to an end . . .' – but not quite, not here at least: Haller is getting on the spot treatment by Germany manager Helmut Schon.

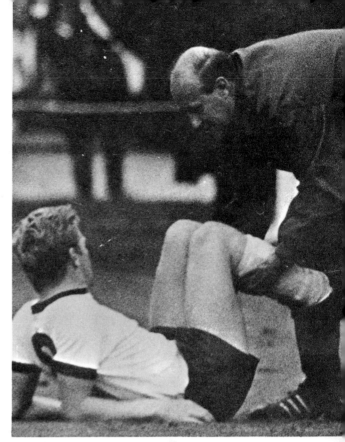

...return to Germany.

I talked to the President. He bluntly refused. 'That's your problem. Why don't you send your wife plus children back home? As for you, you have to stay on. Let there be no mistake about it.'

Our quarrel made headlines in Germany and Italy. I insisted. So did the boss. Finally, he suggested a compromise: the children would get a German private teacher, to be paid by the club.

They meant well. But I did not like the scheme. I was afraid my kids would get silly ideas into their little heads, about being something special and so on. It just did not fit in with my ideas about how to bring up children.

All the same, I had to accept. So here are Karin and Jürgen taking private lessons instead of going to school like ordinary children.

At times, I am brooding about life when I am sitting in my luxuriously furnished flat at Bologna, just 300 yards from the Central Station, where I can watch trains leaving for Germany.

My career started when I joined B.C. Augsburg, the leading football club of my home town in Bavaria, at the age of 9.

Ten years later, Germany's famous coach Sepp Herberger invited me to join the national team. I had received much praise in the papers, and everybody seemed enthusiastic about my technique when playing the ball. So, finally, I had caught the eye of Germany's Grand Old Man of Soccer.

September 24, 1958, was the day of all days. For the first time, I was to play for Germany, versus Denmark, at Copenhagen. However, we did not take the Danes seriously enough. So at the end we were glad to escape with a 1–1 draw.

A prominent German sports journal honoured me with a rather friendly commentary about my first appearance for Germany:

'If young Helmut Haller will not allow himself to be spoiled by flattering comments, this pleasant and unassuming boy will have a great future in Soccer. We hope he will remember this advice.

'At present, he is still lacking confidence and responsibility in critical situations.

'So he should never have missed the opportunity to score the goal which would have given Germany a 2–1 lead and, almost certainly, have meant victory.

'He should rather have risked a shot himself instead of just making another one of those passes . . .

'His technique, however, is brilliant, his tricks and turns are unexpected and surprising, his passes exact. Haller possesses all the qualities required from an outstanding player.'

I have never forgotten these words of praise written about my first performance for Germany. But it was not before my tenth international match that I reached top form, when we played Greece in a World Cup-tie at Athens in September, 1960.

I was really lucky to score what I think was a beautiful goal, and everything went well this time. My streak of bad luck had come to an end, at last. I was invited to join Germany's national team in the 1962 World Cup in Chile.

213 times I had played for my home club, F.C. Augsburg, when I signed a two-year contract with F.C. Bologna, following a magnificent financial offer.

'They are keeping me in a golden cage' – Haller in action for Bologna against fellow German star Karl-Heinz Schnellinger, of Milan.

At that time, I did not even have a banking account of my own. So when they paid out 300,000 marks in cash on signing the contract, I handed the money to my father-in-law right away. He just squeezed all the blue 100 DM notes into his bag, and took them back to Germany.

There, I invested the money in twenty flats and eight garages at Augsburg. I have always made a point of investing my money well and safely.

At Bologna, I had a great start. In a cup-tie against F.C. Torino, on December 5, 1962, I scored four goals. This did not prevent us from losing 6–5! – Certainly no fault of mine.

In 1964, Bologna won the Italian Championship. At Verona, I was awarded the 'Golden Football' by a well-known Soccer journal for being one of the best forwards in Italy.

There is another highlight in my career which I shall never forget. Remember that day in July, 1966, when Germany played England in the World Cup Final at Wembley?

I got the thrill of a lifetime when I scored an early lead for Germany by tricking England's Ray Wilson and surprising Gordon Banks with a shot in the far corner.

This goal certainly came as a shock to a stunned English crowd of 90,000. *Finally, we lost to the luckier, if not better, side that day.*

I am still keeping a souvenir of that day in my home at Bologna. It has been a secret so far, but I will disclose it today: I pinched the ball with which we played the Wembley Final, and I've got it well locked away, for it is more precious to me than any other trophy I have ever won.

Of course, there have been occasional set-backs in my career, and my form has not always been A1.

Once, I was fined 5,000 marks by my club because I had been an utter failure at a match. On another occasion, I was sent off the field for an alleged foul. The referee accused me of having kicked another player. This was certainly not true. Fair play has always been a principle to me.

On the whole, I cannot complain about life in Italy. People are kind and full of admiration.

If I go shopping in Bologna, shopkeepers refuse to accept money from me. 'Get us one more goal next week-end, that's worth more than those few hundred lire,' they say at the greengrocer's or at the cafeteria. If they recognise me in the street, they greet me with enthusiasm: 'Viva 'elmut 'aller' – dropping 'them there H's', like true Cockneys.

Italy's Soccer fans call me '*il ragazzo d'oro*', which means 'The Golden Boy', while the girls prefer to address me as '*il blondino*', meaning 'the blond one'.

It is true, nowhere else in Europe could I lead a better life, nowhere else could I make more money by doing nothing but play football.

However, the time has come for me to return to Germany. There are just a few years left for me in professional Soccer, and I would like to spend them with a German club, preferably in Munich.

'The fans call me il ragazzo d'oro, which means "The Golden Boy"' – Haller takes a break, but there's no break from those keen autograph fans!

DODDY'S HERE!

★

by KEN DODD
Britain's favourite funny man

'VE always been a Soccer fan – ever since me Grandad came to see me play when I was a schoolboy and, after the match, gave me a box f chocolates with the words: 'Here's a box of soft entres for the softest centre I've ever seen. . . .'

Actually I was very keen on the game at school – passed a scholarship for the Holt High School in iverpool, and Liverpool is a football-crazy City if ver I saw one. I played for the school team and as even made captain. I generally played centre-rward and we managed to get to the school nter-League Final, which was played at Anfield.

Short note here for folk who've spent their entire ves living in caves in Outer Mongolia: Anfield is ie home of Liverpool F.C. Come to that, it's the ome of all that is best in football. Come to that, en Outer Mongolians should know about it.

And let me tell you a tattiphilarious secret. I'm ι official, but unpaid, scout for Liverpool. So I've lways kept up my associations with the place. 'hen I'm travelling round the country with the

Diddy folk, I always try and get to a football match – even if it's on a local park ground.

If I see a young player and I think he has out-standing talent, I make a mental note of his name and, as soon as possible, or even sooner, I send a note, or a telegram, or I phone Bill Shankly and pass along my bit of information.

Outer Mongolians should note that Bill is the guv'nor of Anfield! Otherwise known as King Soccer.

'If I see a young player and I think he has outstanding talent I make a mental note of his name . . .' – Ah, now this is Wilson, Harold, from Downing St. United, having a half-time chat with a lemon . . . Oops! 'that's me!

Bill, of course, takes no notice of my memos and that's why Liverpool are such a good side today. Still, it's the thought that counts.

Working in the theatres and television studios all over the country isn't the fittest way of earning a living, you know. That's why I try and keep as fit as I can: leaping around the stage with a tickling-stick wouldn't bring any approval from a physical training instructor as a way of keeping the muscles toned up.

But I always find players at all the big grounds in the country are only too willing to let you join in the training. Of course, they expect a couple of tickets for the show, but I reckon it's a fair exchange.

I'm still waiting for one of the big clubs to put in a transfer request for me. I think I deserve at least a request – probably I'd suit one of the individualistic sides like Manchester United. Can you hear me, Matt?

After all, I'm the hottest favourite at Knotty A Rovers. We play every Sunday at midnight Pimple Park, Knotty Ash . . . and I can tell you *always* win. That's because we never take on a opponents.

And – Oh yes – there're some marvellous play in the team. We've a great Welsh Diddy-goalkee named Ivor Backache, and a rather green inside-l Taffy Apple. But the greatest of our whole sid our inside-right, Toe-'Em-In Tolston.

But Toe-'Em-In has got ingrowing knocked kne and referees get so confused when they see h move, they blow for a goal as soon as his left elb connects with the ball.

And Oh by Jove! I love the thrill of being a football match. The chewed ice lollies down back of your overcoat; and a visit to the Kop Anfield on a Saturday afternoon is both a less and an education in the poetic and lyri phraseology of an inspired crowd.

'I'm still waiting for one of the big clubs to put in a transfer re for me.'

greatest player in Knotty Ash is our inside-right *Toe-'Em-In on'* – but hang on, don't get excited, this isn't him. No, it's the hilarious Tony Hately of Liverpool with his son Mark. BELOW, hits home a right-Diddy goal against Fulham, with Tony Macedo doing a knees-up!

Yes, football is a great British game. One of our best inventions and something that we should be really proud of exporting.

I'll back Britain on that, because I seriously do think we'd be a much poorer nation without the game. But I only hope that the coming months will see more sportsmanship coming into the game. I think that eleven grown men should be able to play hard and with skill without the referee getting his little black book out and taking names.

After all, when all is said and done, it's still a game, a contest of sporting skill. But the players are only part of the problem when it comes to what ails the game.

I hope we can see an end of all that seat-ripping, bottle-throwing and window-breaking that seems to go on so often in the football excursion trains. It makes me sad enough to read about these things and it makes me downright depressed when I hear that some Liverpool fans are involved in these incidents.

'Short note here for folk who've spent their entire lives living in caves in Outer Mongolia' – of which John Sammels of Arsenal, RIGHT, is not one. He got snow-capped at Highbury! BELOW, I'd like to have shown a picture of Knotty Ash playing in treacle, but Liverpool's Tommy Smith ploughing through the snow and the Ferencvaros defence serves just as well. FAR RIGHT, the splendour of Goodison Park – and Everton 'keeper Gordon West nabs the ball off the flying toes of Burnley's Willie Irvine.

Another shot from that Snowman's Ball at Anfield – Liverpool's Geoff Strong, centre, tries to ski through the Ferencvaros defence in their European Fairs Cup game.

At Knotty Ash, anyone who misbehaves at one of our games is immediately sentenced to seven years' hard luck and hard labour in the treacle mines. That's after they've been patched up at the hospital by Dr. Diddy-Crippen.

No, seriously, I know that football can make people very emotional, and Liverpool, supporting two powerful First Division teams, must be the most football-crazy capital of the country (what-

ever Terry Venables says elsewhere in this annual) but I can't see how it can make people crazy enough to slash a railway-carriage seat after the match has finished.

Meanwhile, I'll be trying again this next season to get Bill Shankly to introduce the 6–2–4 plan at Anfield. Six goals to Liverpool, two against and four each week to the referee.

Tatty-bye!

WHY I'M UNIQUE !

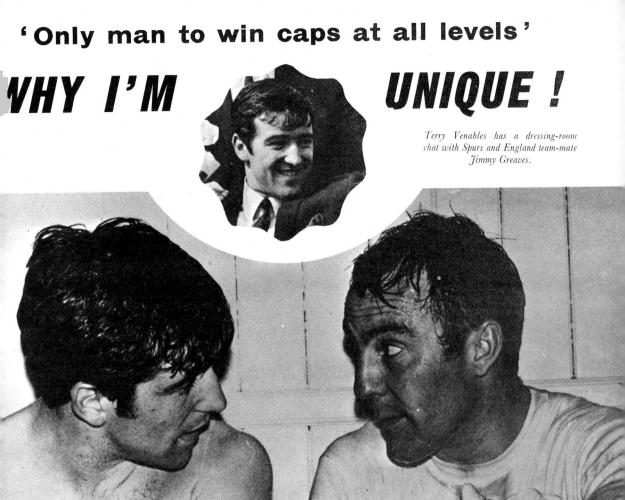

Terry Venables has a dressing-room chat with Spurs and England team-mate Jimmy Greaves.

by TERRY VENABLES
(*of Tottenham Hotspur and England*)

FOOTBALL'S a game, a sport and, for some of us, a profession. To get the most out of it, you've got to play to win. But I'm not too keen on the sheer statistics of it all. I haven't got that mathematical sort of brain that can churn out facts and figures like a computer.

But somebody worked it out that I was a pretty unusual sort of statistic myself. The only Englishman so far to win full international caps at all available five levels: Schools, Youth, Amateur, Under-23 and England. How come there's only one of me who has gone nap? The answer is an ambition that didn't come true.

Here's what happened. The pattern started when I went to a good Soccer school, Lymington Secondary Modern, at Dagenham, in Essex . . . near enough to Bow Bells to make me a Cockney at heart, if not in fact. I started off on the wing, at

the age of 11, learning how to keep out of troubl
in the first team against other blokes who wer
loftier, weightier and about four years older.

Then I played for Dagenham Schools, then Esse
Schools, then England School trials . . . and the
the full England XI. I had six matches, one a
Wembley against the Scots when a red-haired littl
fellow named Billy Bremner was marking me. W
won 3–1.

Stage one of the nap hand over, then. I was wing
half – our forward line: Phil Chisnall, now with
Southend; West Ham's Ronnie Boyce; Bert Murray
once Chelsea now Birmingham City; Liverpool'
great Peter Thompson at inside-forward; and
Jantzen Derrick, Bristol-born, now with City there

And the odd thing about this Schools' side is tha
only I of the defence that year went on to profes
sional football for any length of time. That starry
forward line hogged all the later honours.

Anyway, came stage two. I captained the Youth
side from wing-half – we had eight matches, I
remember, and the point was that I now knew I
wanted to become a professional. So did some of
the others in that Youth team – like Gordon West,
Martin Peters, Ronnie Boyce (he seems to crop up

Keeping a close eye on the action (TOP, LEFT) – *Nottingham Forest's
Frank Wignall and Spurs wing-half Dave Mackay. LEFT, Terry
Venables tangles with star Liverpool winger Peter Thompson.*

everywhere), and Frankie Saul and David Wagstaffe.

I was with Chelsea by then, as a junior. But I knew I was in the running for the England Amateur XI. A couple of pretty good trials and I got my first 'cap'. Now I could have signed pro forms with Chelsea that same year but I hung on, simply because I desperately wanted to get in the England Olympic squad for the Rome Olympics.

Well, the fact is I didn't make it. But what I did make was this odd record of playing at all five levels. Soon as I could after knowing I wasn't getting a 'Roman Holiday', I signed pro and was lucky enough to get straight into the Chelsea first team.

Stage four was being capped for the England Under-23s, first as wing-half and later as inside-forward. And then the full England cap. Now it looks as if it'll be a long time before anyone comes up to join me in this particular statistical section of the game.

Most blokes who are good at the game sign professional forms as soon as they are 17 and it's unusual to get in the amateur side earlier than that. . . .

But what I'd like to do now is put in a good word for the fanaticism of London football as compared with that in the better-known 'hot-spots' like

*A third, crushing goal for Spurs (*TOP*) against Olympique Lyonnaise in their European Cup-winners' Cup match: scorer is Cliff Jones . . . who's also takn a full-length dive.* RIGHT, *is this how Mick McManus would play Soccer? – It's Birmingham's Beard appearing to 'scissor' Spurs' former forward Frank Saul!*

Liverpool-Everton and Rangers-Celtic. Northern fans reckon their sense of rivalry is intense, but in London where there are usually five First Division clubs . . . well, we have our own pocket-sized version of the League Championship.

Derby games between Fulham and Chelsea, or Spurs and Arsenal, have been building tremendously in intensity in recent years. Throw in the 'unpredictables', West Ham, and you've got a tough little competition going on which is private to London.

All right – so it'd be silly to say it's as strong as say Liverpool and Everton, but it's certainly not as tame as some Merseyside fans would have people

believe. It stems, of course, from so many clubs being so close together.

Before a Derby game, you get local fans galore coming up to you and saying: 'Look, I don't care who you lose to this season but you've *got* to beat that local mob on Saturday – otherwise I'll never be able to look the blokes at work in the face again.'

So it builds up. We have maybe ten London Derby games a year and the fans keep their own table of results affecting only London clubs . . . and their enthusiasm comes through to the players. London supporters are as loyal as those anywhere in the British Isles – and I'm not saying that just because I'm a Londoner or because London has

been the centre of my Soccer life.

I remember one game very well indeed. I was about 18 and playing for Chelsea *against* Spurs . . . little did I know that later on I'd have a switch of playing loyalties and turn out for Spurs against Chelsea in the F.A. Cup Final at Wembley (which Spurs won 2–1, by the way!).

But in this particular Derby game, we were a goal up and going nicely against all the odds and the tipsters and the experts. Then the Chelsea (now West Ham) winger Peter Brabrook busted his collarbone in a tackle. Spurs levelled at 1–1. Bobby Smith scored it.

Just on half-time the Chelsea ten men went to 2–1 up and we really played marvellously well. But in the dying minutes Terry Medwin and Maurice Norman scored to give Spurs the points. A Derby game to remember – it had everything.

And many London 'locals' are like that.

Actually in that game Jimmy Greaves was also with Chelsea. Just shows the amount of switching around there is inside the London area alone.

What I'm trying to pinpoint, though, is simply that it's not true that there isn't the enthusiasm in London. There *is*. And that despite the fact that so many of the players are matey with those of the other sides. We rate our supporters highly. Just makes me mad to hear London fans put down as being a molly-coddled lot with no fire in their 'tums'.

And don't let people tell you that London-based players are dazzled by the bright lights of the Big City. They're too busy trying to live up to the ambitious ideals of their supporters. Cockney wit is just as cutting as Liverpool 'Koppisms' or Manchester mud-slinging or Scottish sarcasm. I know. I've sampled all of it.

'There's tremendous enthusiasm for the London Derby games . . .' – West Ham's Peter Brabrook (right) looks horrified as he loses the ball to Arsenal's Furnell and Simpson.

ONLY FIGHT FOR BALL THAT CAN BE WON

by RON GREENWOOD
(Manager of West Ham)

POSSESSION of the ball is vital in football. Without the ball we can only defend and real football is based on attack, so it follows that somehow we must win the ball.

In Britain it seems to be universally accepted that the only way to win the ball is in the tackle and everyone is urged to get stuck in. People often say things like, 'He's a good player, he tackles hard. He goes right through his opponent to get the ball.'

It seems to be accepted that getting 'stuck-in' is

manly, but in all honesty how can a player g through his opponent and comply with the Law of the game?

Continental players have in general a muc better appreciation of the value of interceptio If you win possession by interception you are o your feet and can use the ball to start an attack.

They also accept that when a good player ha possession it is almost impossible to tackle him suc cessfully. They are content to hold him up an cover the passing angles open to him.

Even in the tackle many of them have a techniqu which is different from that of the British, wh throw out a foot and are satisfied if the ball goe into touch. They try to remain standing and the support the tackling foot with the body.

The foot is easily evaded by good players but th body is a far bigger obstruction than the foot an not so easily evaded.

Only as a last resort are the good players satisfied to pu the ball into touch. They base their game on winning th ball and using it to start an attack.

It is best to try to cultivate a better appreciatio

'This competitiveness is Britain's greatest asset and one which the re of the world envies' – Here England's (and West Ham's) Geoff Hur. shows it off against Russia at Wembley. It's a fifty-fifty ball – it's Hurst thigh against the Russian's neck, with the ball precariously between . .

of the use of the body and an awareness of the role the body plays in playing the ball. Obstruction is better than kicking. Using the body is always better than using the boot.

I'm not condemning the British way of playing, but we must accept that there is an in-between, an ideal, balanced between the two styles. We go through our opponents to win the ball, they stand off because they know they can't win it.

We must learn to pick out the ball we can win and the ball we can't and if players do this we will not need referees to intervene.

Getting 'stuck-in' to players like George Best of Manchester United is fatal. He is too good to be beaten in a reckless tackle.

Tackle a winger like Best from behind, as he is going through and it is a foul. Tackle him from behind when the ball is laid up to him and it is OK. But either way it is a foul, for you cannot win the ball from behind a good player without going 'through him'.

Continental players will grant possession to you in situations like this, where the ball is laid up to you. At throw-ins for example good players know it's impossible to win the ball, but others go in and have fouls given against them.

Factors like this will be vitally important when the next World Cup series is played in Mexico. In 1966 the series was dominated by Nordic-type teams who played the hard-running, get 'stuck-in' kind of game.

Such a high work rate will be impossible in Mexico, where the effects of the altitude can rapidly reduce a player to a state of exhaustion. *The Mexico World Cup will be won by players who know when they cannot win the ball and can conserve their energy.*

Intelligent players learn to read angles that can be used by a player in possession and under pressure. The opponent can only use those limited angles and, knowing in advance what he will do, we can intercept.

At West Ham we recently had two Finnish players training with us for four months. The President of their club, H.J.K., sent them here and paid all their expenses. Watching their development has been very interesting for me.

In terms of skill the two Finns are better than most of our players. Last season they played in the European Cup Winners' Cup against Polish Cup holders Wisla Krakow, but they've been brought up to play the game at their own pace.

When they arrived from Finland they had no appreciation of the speed of our game and, above all, no awareness of people around them who want

'You cannot win the ball from behind a good player without going "through him"' – Skipping out of such trouble is West Ham's new star, Redknapp, against Arsenal.

win the ball regardless.

Slowly they learned that if you lay the ball off quickly you automatically get space. They learned to use their skills in the face of quick tackling and acquired an awareness of other players.

Before these two returned to Finland they were vastly improved. They had learned to play at the speed of the English game and also acquired some of our competitiveness.

This competitiveness is Britain's greatest asset and one which the rest of the world envies.

Our players rise to the challenge of a true fifty-fifty ball but they have not yet recognised that a forty-sixty ball demands intelligence. How much better it would be if our competitive spirit was tempered by intelligence.

When to be competitive is the vital factor in winning the ball, for we must always fight for the ball which can be won, but recognise that we cannot win every ball.

'Our players rise to the challenge of a true fifty-fifty ball. . . .' – It's Geoff Hurst on the rise here (left), but this time he was beaten by Russia's 'keeper Psenitchuikov.

JOHN COHEN

We're less human than we think

by PROFESSOR JOHN COHEN

(*Head of the Department of Psychology the University of Manchester*)

John Cohen . . . 'Misuse of energy'

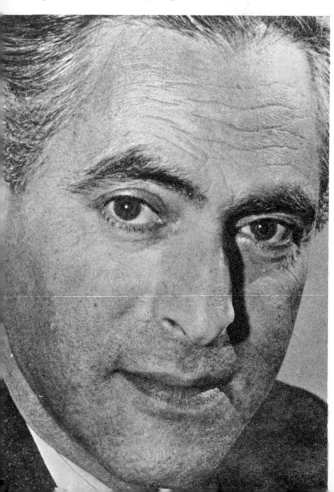

the pr VIOl

FOOTBALL is one of the most refined and sublimated forms of organised aggression that man has invented, because in theory violence is directed against the ball and not against man. But that rule is now being denied by events.

Where does all this human aggressiveness, in football or anywhere else, come from? Part is inborn. If Man had been completely devoid of any aggressive impulse he would long ago have become extinct.

In football the energy concentrated in the leg and aimed at the ball can, at the slightest encouragement, turn into a vicious assault against another player.

Football reveals how much less human we all are than we imagine ourselves to be. Take the injured player. He is, perhaps, in great pain, but in the crowd there is no feeling of compassion, only: '*We are wasting time!*'

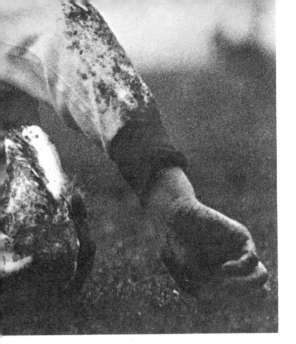

Action from FIFA, not just words

by LEO HORN

(Holland's World-famous referee)

Leo Horn . . . 'Who backs referees?'

lem of

ENCE

THE biggest contributing factor behind the present wave of violence in football is the attitude of the clubs. There isn't enough discipline anywhere, on the playing pitches or on the terraces. And when someone attemps to impose order and discipline, the general attitude is that they must be wrong.

Among the fans, the majority are younger than they used to be, many between 16 and 20 years. Every country has its share of hooligans but no one yet has done anything about them. The hooligans control the terraces and the players dominate the referees!

Referees today are not strong enough. Afraid of the big stars, they are too easy on the players. But it would be unfair to blame the referees for this state of affairs. I know very well that the present attitude is that if you send off a star player an influential

JOHN COHEN

Part of aggressive behaviour comes by imitation or as a response to frustration. Turning the other cheek is easier said than done. Most people prefer to lash out.

Sometimes it's violence with the tongue – swearing has brought punishment to many a British footballer, and in Italy swearing brings a fine of £3 per word, £11 for swearing at the referee.

Sex is another factor. As Freud remarked, it may be that nothing important can occur in a person without in some way invoking a degree of 'sexualisation'.

Since sex and aggression are closely link violence will more readily burst out when a play is caught up body and soul in the heat of the gan

The satisfactions which players derive from fo ball seem to bear some likeness to the sequence pleasures in sex. There is the foreplay, the mounti tension and finally an explosive climax.

When a goal is scored there is a vast detumesce relief. No wonder the word 'sport' once mea 'amorous dalliance'.

Anyone keyed to a high pitch of excitement c fly into a fury if things go wrong. There is a psych logical law to that effect. The more absorbing t task in which a person (or player) is engaged t

'THE PUNCH-UP' (LEFT) *was the famous one between Arsenal's Ian Ure and Manchester United's Denis Law, at Old Trafford. It led to scenes similar to the one above. And then, almost inevitably, to the scene below – Law leading off Ure, after both had been given their marching orders . . .*

LEO HORN

club might see to it that your name disappears from the League list at the end of the season!

All over the world the leagues and national associations are letting the referees down. They are not standing behind them, firmly, as they should. The referees know very well what the situation is. Now the referee hopes to finish a game with 22 players on the field, for he knows that bad reports from the clubs mean good-bye to the referee's future.

When a player is sent off by the referee, the player makes excuses and the club claims the referee made a mistake. *No club yet has ever said, 'Yes, the referee was right, our player is guilty.'*

Having been a referee for 32 years I've seen the growing influence of money within the game. Prior to 1954 the Dutch game was all amateur, and until around that time the maximum wage in England was between £20 and £30 a week.

I refereed the England–Belgium game at Wembley back in 1952, and three times I controlled 'needle' matches between England and Scotland. For me that was a great honour indeed, and I can say a great pleasure, too. In those days the players concentrated on playing football and the referee's job was comparatively easy.

With the growth of the big international competitions since 1954, more and more money has come into the game. Dutch champions Ajax for example have made more than £100,000 from their European Cup games and the money made in Latin countries is often fantastic. Paying £100 a week or more to the top stars, the big clubs cannot afford to lose.

All the violence began with the growth of the European Cup into big business. Real Madrid, Manchester United, Celtic – and more clubs who've made big names in the European Cup – started the rough game!

Unless something is done quickly a great many

JOHN COHEN

nore readily he is frustrated and explodes in anger.

Violence in football is not due to one cause alone nor is the remedy a simple one. Nor is the answer to tamper with the system and hope for the best.

For example, to forbid singing and chanting might only lead to bigger trouble, because all that exuberance may look for more direct and dangerous outlets.

Nor do I share Sir Stanley Rous's opinion that tickets should be issued through schoolmasters, youth leaders and sports organisers only to people they know to be responsible.

That might be all right for football as such. But those who are debarred might well take it out on the community as a whole.

As the police well know, a crowd is different from a collection of individuals. An individual is trans-

LEO HORN

referees will give up the game. Look at the situation from their point of view.

In many countries referees are forbidden to write in newspapers or give interviews. They cannot appear on television without first getting permission in writing! Players and clubs can say what they want about referees, but the referee must remain silent.

In Holland referees receive a meagre £8 a game. In England £10 10s. and in West Germany they get nothing at all. For £8 a week and all the headaches,

---

'European Cup began it all'

formed when he becomes part of a crowd.

As a member of a crowd, he loses his identity. He is anonymous but part of the power of the crowd. The emotional element takes over from the thinking element.

That's why mobs are fickle and volatile. They are easily moved to assault, destruction, looting and even, as U.S. experience has shown, to lynching.

A law-abiding spectator may conduct himself quite differently when he is infected by so-called

I gave it up. Until referees are paid enough to live on and until they receive active support from the authorities, the game will continue to slide.

This doesn't mean that referees are never offered big money, but they are not allowed to take it. Some years ago I was invited to South America to control a South American Champions Cup Final between Santos (Brazil) and Penarol. When the tie ended all square a third game had to be played and I was asked to stay on for it.

In goes John Kaye of West Bromwich Albion – but the picture's stolen by high-leaping Southampton 'keeper Forsyth, who collects Kaye's header safely.

JOHN COHEN

An image of '68 – Eight policemen are required to hustle off a troublesome Liverpool fan at Craven Cottage. 'An individual is transformed when he becomes part of a crowd,' comments Professor Cohen.

mob hysteria. Crowd behaviour is a form of epidemic. An emotional rash spreads like lightning through a vast crowd.

It's possible that the anonymity which stamps a crowd is more marked away from home. If so, an 'away' crowd is more ungovernable than a 'home' crowd – as British Rail can no doubt witness.

How does the alleged indiscipline of star players affect supporters?

Ardent fans identify themselves with their heroes. If the hero is a law unto himself and defies his manager and the referee the fans take a cue from him.

His defiance, bad language and violence will make legal their own rowdyism. What's more, a threat to the prestige of the hero is taken personally by his fans, who're already at a fever pitch of excitement.

That has a wider application than football. The fans of a pop singer would be ready to tear his 'enemy' limb from limb.

A tougher line by directors and managers might well be a healthy move. Another would be to provide civilised accommodation for spectators in place of the primitive facilities available in most places.

If people are treated like human beings they are more likely to behave as such.

Also, those in control could upgrade the status of the referee. A referee is a witness, jury, judge and policeman rolled into one. His prestige – and salary, too – in relation to the players should be determined by his most important role, namely that of a judge.

To pro footballers the role of referee as judge renders him just as important a factor as the opposing team. It's common for the virtues and vices of a referee to be analysed by players before a game, particularly abroad.

It's natural for a team to feel some coolness towards a strange referee, specially if he appears aloof. Much could be done by a friendly chat between him and them before the match.

We are dealing with a situation, violence in football, about which we do not know enough. Its sources are obscure and the way to control it is in doubt. How could we regulate a central-heating system if we didn't know where the heat came from or how to keep it from exceeding a given level?

By and large, violence in football is not really crime, even when planned in advance. It is the misuse and misdirection of too much energy and should be treated as such. This does not exclude penalties for breaking the law.

We are faced with a breakdown in the sport of football because it is subjected to too much strain. The hooligans are indulging in more emotions than they are able to bear. But to rely on penalties and selection of spectators may possibly breed worse evils.

None the less, my crystal ball tells me that the greatest days of football are yet to come.

LEO HORN

After the play-off, in which the players had been

EO HORN

...aying for $3,000 a man, the Secretary of the Sud...mericana Federation handed me an envelope. 'hat,' he said, 'will take care of your expenses.' I ...oked inside and found $1,000 and immediately ...nded it back. Under the rules I was allowed 60 ...wiss francs per day – for my seven days abroad, ...ound £35.

Only U.E.F.A. and F.I.F.A. are in a position to ...tablish uniformity. But despite many problems in ...e competitions they control, F.I.F.A. has so far ...one nothing but talk.

It was clear to me after the 1962 World Cup that ...outh American players are quite different in tem...erament from their European counterparts. Many ...outh Americans are real comedians – highly skilled ...ctors who are very good at 'falling' down and pre...ending injury. Argentinians, Italians, Spaniards ...nd Greeks are all different and World Cup referees ...ust have broad experience of handling them all.

Seven times I was invited to Greece to handle top ...eague games, and believe me the game in Greece ...different. If ever a Greek referee was appointed to ...andle a European Cup-tie between an English and

a West German team, believe me he would be in real trouble.

I explained all this to Sir Stanley Rous soon after I handled the 1962 World Cup game between Russia and Chile. My suggestion was that F.I.F.A. should arrange regular exchanges of referees for league games, taking the best five officials from each country. I also complained that in Chile the official referees had been allocated one room between three.

Between 1962 and 1966 F.I.F.A. did nothing to solve the problems. Sir Stanley Rous talked of the problems often, but he did nothing. Nothing, that is, except to see to it that for the 1966 World Cup Finals the referees had a room each – and that Leo Horn was not on the list of referees.

Since my retirement, many Dutch people have asked me why, in view of my long experience, I was not on the Dutch Referees' Committee. Until very recently I could offer no explanation, but not long ago the Royal Dutch F.A. Vice-President told me the reason.

It would be an insult, he said . . . to Sir Stanley Rous!

' saw that!' – Referee Nicholson jabs the whistle to his mouth as ...oventry's Morrissey brings down Sheffield Wednesday's John Fantham, right.

SPLENDOUR DEDICATE

'Fouls used coldly as instrument of policy'

by BRIAN GLANVILLE

(*Novelist, and* Sunday Times *football writer*)

WHAT with the disgraceful episodes of the Celtic–Racing World Club Final matche and Pelé's professed intention not to compete in the 1970 World Cup, there have been sign that football may be set on a collision course; that international competition may sink in a welter violence.

It has all long gone far beyond a joke, just Soccer itself has long transcended – or falle beneath – the limits of a game. The circumstanc of Pelé's renunciation are worth examining, th more so as he himself has been the advocate retaliatory violence as a means of pacifying aggre sive defenders.

Vicente Feola, Brazil's team manager, advise him on these lines, he says, in 1959, and he has bee grateful ever since. Yet his determination not play in 1970 – my own feeling is that he will chang his mind – indicates that the policy has been u successful.

It did not, after all, prevent him from bein kicked out of the 1966 World Cup, first by Zetche of Bulgaria, then by the still more ruthless Morai

On each occasion, Pelé had pitifully little prote tion from a weak English referee. The Morais fou will stick in the mind of all who saw them, either i actuality, or in the film 'GOAL!', when a 'froze frame' allowed one to see them in all their brut premeditation.

Spurs' Cliff Jones, bloodied, his head gashed, is helped off – 'There a signs that football is on a collision course,' says Brian Glanville.

'The violence involved is essentially motiveless, free-floating violence, looking for an outlet and an opportunity' – One such opportunity seemed to be afforded by this young Manchester United fan, being treated for a head wound at Bramall-lane.

achieve, when it goes to work on sufficiently combustible material. There can be no excuse, though there may be valid explanations, for the behaviour of some of the Celtic players in the play-off in Montevideo; for Hughes first punching then kicking the Racing goalkeeper, for Gemmell running up to kick an opponent, for Auld assaulting another.

But, by the same token, Cejas, the assaulted goalkeeper, had himself run forty yards to kick little Johnstone in the ribs when he was lying injured – under the guise of commiserating with him, while Johnstone, at half-time, was obliged to wash the spittle out of his hair.

This disgusting habit – one Racing player, Rodrigues, early in the game in Montevideo, deliberately spat in the face of all four Celtic back-line defenders – is proof enough that Racing were bent on provocation. And when one reaches this point, one asks oneself whether the game is worth the candle. What earthly object is there in playing these matches at all when certain countries approach them as they would approach a war?

Violence by spectators comes into another category; or rather, into two categories. One must differentiate between the sort of barbarism which has been traditional, say, at Rangers–Celtic matches throughout the century, the sort of violence which led to 44 deaths at a Turkish Second Division match in September, 1967, and the kind which leads spectators to set about one another on the terraces.

This last phenomenon has, in essence, nothing to do with football at all; it has simply chosen football as its context. The violence involved is essentially motiveless, free-floating violence, looking for an outlet and an opportunity. It might be regarded as the revenge of ungifted, 'underprivileged' youth on an affluent society which has no real place for them.

Peter Terson's lively and interesting musical play, *Zigger Zagger*, so well performed by the National Youth Theatre in 1967, summed it up perfectly. Zigger Zagger himself, half-Pan, half-Machiavelli, the malign sprite of the terraces behind the City

Pelé himself was deeply influenced by the film; he has said that until he watched it, he was prepared to believe that the fouls had been unintentional. In that case, the poor fellow must have been the only man in Goodison Park that evening to think so.

As for the Racing–Celtic Finals, they were an example of what cynical provocation can finally

has all long gone far beyond a joke' – and international referee George
cCabe looks as if he'd share that opinion, after an incident in an
English League game . . .

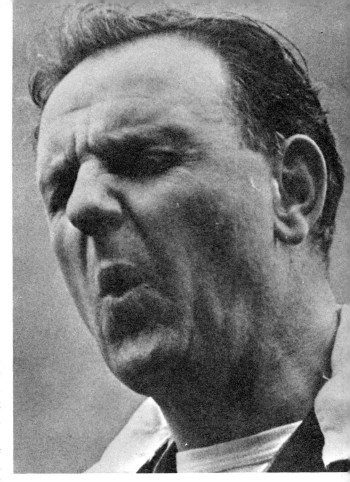

al, has this to say: 'Full time. And we've made
em. Spurred them on again. That's me moment.
Vhen that final whistle goes and we've won. That's
iumph. Then I go for me tea, listen to the final
sults on telly, and out for the Saturday night
ooze-up and looking for foreign supporters to
ash up.'

The psychopathic lout who threw a stone at
eltic's goalkeeper, Ronnie Simpson, in Buenos
ires, putting him out of the match before a ball
as kicked, was another kind of mental defective.
Vhile Zigger's identification with his team is whole-
earted and important, his dedication to violence is
ist as great, or greater. But the Argentinian's
iolent action had a definite purpose, over and
bove itself. It was not a gratuitous action.

A few days after the events of Montevideo, I found
myself involved in a discussion on Italian television
ith Juan Carlos Lorenzo, manager of the Argen-
nian World Cup side which played in England in
966. Lorenzo was soft-pedalling; he deprecated the
iterviewer's suggestion that any mutual animus
as left over from the England–Argentina game at
Vembley, and when I said that the present World
hampionship system of home and away games,
llowed so closely by a play-off, was mistaken, he
lleged that there had been no trouble when
ndependiente twice contested the Final against
nternazionale.

I replied that in 1965, four Inter. players and
Ielenio Herrera, their manager, had been hit by
nissiles in Buenos Aires, so that all one could justly
ay was that the aim of the Argentinian fan was
ecoming more accurate. I also pointed out that,
s one who admired the technical ability of the
Argentinian footballer, it was still true to say that
t Wembley, as in Montevideo, they had shown a
isturbing cynicism; one which, in Montevideo,
ad had its response in terms of brutality.

Lorenzo himself admitted that Argentinian foot-
all had latterly become more robust and defensive.
But any neutral person who was present at the
Vembley game, I feel, would agree that Argentina's
nethods turned the match into a travesty. It was
ot that they were especially vicious; simply that
hey used the foul coldly, as an instrument of policy.
f an English forward beat an Argentinian defender,

he had a better than even chance of being stopped
by illegal methods; by being held, tripped or pushed.

In the circumstances, the England players kept
their temper very well, but when Antonio Rattin
was sent off by Herr Kreitlein for *'the look in his eye'*
– as Lorenzo with some bitterness recalled – there
was a certain rough justice about it. Rattin, as
captain, had in some degree emerged as the symbol
of what the Argentinian team were about that
afternoon: a splendid footballer dedicated to anti-
football.

I have painted a depressing, negative picture, but
there are, here and there, glimmers of light. Empiri-
cally, it can be shown that important matches don't
have to be ill-tempered, ruthless, blood-and-iron
affairs. The World Cup Final between England
and Germany, for example, produced a game without a serious foul, despite the colossal tension. And,

107

eltic's Jimmy Johnstone flies out of trouble under the determined tackle
of a Dukla defender.

'It can be shown that important matches don't have to be ill-tempered, ruthless, blood-and-iron affairs' – but meanwhile many of them are: remember this shot from the European Cup Final, with Celtic's Jock Stein (left) about to make a protest, and Inter.'s Helenio Herrera trying to restrain him?

if the match between England and Italy at Highbury in 1934 is still known as the Battle of Highbury for its notorious imbroglio, the match in which England beat Italy 4–0 at Turin in 1948 was a very different story. 'You had to admire those fellows,' Laurie Scott, the England right-back that day, said to me years afterwards. 'Even when their tails were between their legs, they never did anything nasty.'

The World Cup has been producing its brawls ever since it was initiated, in 1930, when the Argentinians and the Mexicans had a set-to in Montevideo. In 1938, the worst example of brawling was provided by a match between the Czechs and the Brazilians. But since then, international competition has become a great deal more tense, exacerbated by trends towards more and more defensive football.

Poor refereeing, as we know, is often at the bottom of the worst examples. When a referee is weak or inadequate, players already on edge, slip over the edge, into violence. If they do not think a referee is capable of giving them protection from ill usage,

they will take the law into their own hands. Ther can also be games which are, as Mr. Ken Asto termed the game he tried to referee between Chil and Italy in the 1962 World Cup, 'Uncontrollable That is to say, if neither side has the intention t play football, but is more concerned with wreakin physical harm on the opposite side, there is littl that even the best referee in the world can do.

The position is complicated by the chauvinism c certain national bodies. One will long remembe the disingenuous statement put out by one of th Portuguese officials after Pelé had been so cruell fouled at Everton. Pelé, he blithely said, appeare to have been injured. Portugal themselves shoul have suspended Morais, just as Racing, instead c giving their delinquent players a bonus, shoul have followed the example of Celtic, and fine them.

A possible solution lies in the strengthening c F.I.F.A. as a disciplinary body, meting out justic and condign punishment where it appears necessar But the prospects are perturbing.

UNIVERSAL ATHLETES WILL INHERIT GAME

by JOSEF MASOPUST
(Dukla-Prague and Czechoslovakia)

former European Footballer of the Year

I HAVE recently started my eighteenth season in the First Division. Soccer changed considerably during those eighteen years in Czechoslovakia and also, apparently, in other countries.

I remember for instance how we practised in 1950, when I first put on the First Division shirt in Teplice. What a difference from the present. We practised only three times a week, whereas players today practise practically every day.

However, technique has not improved at the same rate. It is much harder to control the ball when running quickly than when moving relatively slowly. Hence fast Soccer often loses its accuracy, and people remembering old times are convinced that better Soccer was played before the Second World War.

I cannot agree with that. I will only admit that pre-war Soccer could have been more attractive for spectators.

One more thing changed during my eighteen years as a Soccer player. The coach usually made only very few comments before a match, as for instance: 'Keep your eye on Pavlovic, he is a very good shooter!' or 'Try to play through the wings. They have Vican playing centre-half, you cannot pass that way', and so on.

Every player today going on the field has his exact orders and role and is thus limited. A Soccer player may lose his independent thinking and pleasure from the game when fulfilling accurately tactical orders, but this system may fully satisfy players without any individualism.

It allows even technically not very skilled players to play perfectly their defence roles. Therefore, most teams choose one of the various defence systems when playing a better team. So-called 'concrete defence' is usually played in away matches,

without regard to the fact that both teams are approximately similar quality. This can be observe in Czechoslovakia and most other countries at cl level and in two-leg European Champions C matches.

These defence tendencies have brought voices proclaimi that Soccer will not survive a period longer than forty fifty years at most.

Statistics have showed a decrease in goals score in European Soccer and, consequently, in numbe of spectators. Such voices rather depress me, spite of the fact that Soccer's survival for anoth fifty years is not of great personal consequence me. I shall probably have other worries at th time, if any at all.

In Czechoslovakia – as well as in several oth countries – both coaches and players have be blamed for this defensive play, which it is assert deprives Soccer of its beauty. However, Soccer played for points (and money) and not for beaut

I found it even during our European Champio Cup Semi-Final with Glasgow Celtic in Pragu Celtic are a great team and demonstrated the quality by the Final victory in Lisbon.

However, in Prague, the Scottish players co centrated on defence, this resulting in a 0–0 scor The attacking players did not even try to sho when having the ball, but tried to get it to a corn and keep it there as long as possible. The spectato were disappointed; it was not an attractive gam However, the system gave the required resu Nothing can be done against it.

I do not believe that the problem of defensi systems can be solved by any change of rules. T offside rule has been fairly extensively discuss recently. Many reformers proposed an abolition this rule. Others suggested at least a partial chang

In my opinion, such attempts are not justifi and are not likely to bring about improvement. A abolition of the offside rule would complete change the character of Soccer, and create completely different game.

We made a trial, and played a training matc with the offside rule suspended. Many goals we scored but believe me, the game was not good, an I am sure that spectators would not like it at al Moreover, who knows whether even under altere

A fine action shot of Manchester City's Ken Mulhearn palming a shot over the bar as Everton's Alan Ball challenges.

Peter Bonetti flails in, Eddie McCreadie's 'at the ready' (background and it adds up to a wasted effort by Coventry City's Ronnie Rees . .

TOP, *a touch of the 'Brazil bicycle kick' from Liverpool's Ian St. John against Coventry.* BELOW, *it's a 'hands and knees' Leicester defence keeping out this header from Coventry's Ian Gibson (on left).* FACING PAGE, *Wolves' Derek Dougan (No. 9) is also 'hands and knees' but his desperate tackle didn't prevent this shot from Sheffield Wednesday centre-half Ellis . . .*

rules a defensive system would not be created which would detract from the beauty of Soccer more than the present system.

As a matter of fact they are especially in trouble with defence in Italy, although in the system of so-called 'free stopper' offside is practically not observed.

Making the goalmouth bigger is also often discussed. Sir Stanley Matthews, during his visit to Czechoslovakia, supported this idea. It is evident that the skill of goalkeepers has improved considerably during the last hundred years, when the exact size of Soccer goals was established. Nowadays the goalmouth is relatively small, for good goalkeepers. The suggested goal enlargement should not be substantial, or it would result in a search for giant goalkeepers.

All discussions concerning changes of the Soccer rules have one common aim: to increase the number of goals scored. However, I do not think that a change of Soccer rules alone would be useful. Besides, Soccer is not in serious danger; nobody any longer claims that it will not survive.

Personally, I am convinced that Soccer will nev lose its attraction. On the contrary, modern Socc will bring more beauty and excitement than present. The players of the future will be average better skilled than my generation.

Forceful Soccer based on perfect physical co dition characterises football in Europe. The physic condition of most leading European Soccer playe has practically reached its maximum and ca hardly be improved. However, their technical skil that is, heading, controlling the ball with both fe shooting, etc., can be improved. Even leadi players have further scope in this respect.

The Soccer player of the future should be a u versal athlete, that is, he should be tough, in exc lent physical shape but should also possess a perfe technique, be smart, and have creative abilities a a feeling for teamwork.

Such players will play not only fast and toug but also technical and intelligent Soccer; and tha the type of Soccer in which I believe.

In rip-roaring action . . . Nottingham Forest's highly-valued Welsh international half-back Terry Hennessey fighting off Stoke forward Mahoney.

HOW TO CRACK
'CATENACCIO'

by KURT HAMRIN

(of A.C. Milan and Sweden)

A LOT of water has passed under the bridge since that day in 1956 when as a 22-year-old amateur with A.I.K. I left my native Sweden and flew out to Italy to sign on as a professional for Juventus of Turin.

The Soccer revolution in Italy which was to impose the iron grip of the '*catenaccio*' defence on all tactical thinking had not yet begun. It is no coincidence that my best goal-scoring seasons during my eleven-year career in Italy were in 1958 and 1959, when I notched up 26 goals in each.

The effect of '*catenaccio*' tactics was startling, for although I have kept my position among the leading three or four in the annual list of scorers, my average over the past seven years has been between 14 and 18 goals.

Incredible though it may seem, this 14–18 goal average, which would seem trivial in a country such as England, has been just as productive in points for my club as those 'respectable' totals in 1958–59.

For under the present defensive system an extremely high percentage of matches are won with a 1–0 scoreline and 14 goals in a season can easily win more than 20 points in the final League table.

In fact I regard the 1966–67 season in which I scored 16 goals as one of the most successful I have had since coming to Italy.

Luigi Riva of Cagliari topped the list with 18 goals, followed by Inter.-Milan's Sandro Mazzola with 17. José Altafini of Naples and myself were third.

But though the '*catenaccio*' severely restricts the number of goals scored, it has its weaknesses and I

mobility, speed, unpredictability'

consider I have not been altogether unsuccessful in exploiting them.

Its strength is its meticulously planned pattern with rigid man-to-man marking, and paradoxically this is also one of its weaknesses. For if you can throw one part of the pattern out of line, you also disrupt the whole.

Mobility, speed and, above all, unpredictability, are the weapons I have tried to perfect against that wall of defenders which meets every attacking move.

Knowing where to position yourself and what to do, with or without the ball, is instinctive. You don't really think much beforehand. You don't have time.

When I go roaming over to the left wing there is no fixed plan behind it. It is part of being mobile. Of course I know that invariably the back marking me will follow and while the rest of the defence are adjusting positions deep in their own half they are most vulnerable.

But this is the effect of a move which is carried out instinctively and not planned for that purpose specifically.

Speed is a vital part in this concept which I have formed in making the opposition shuffle the cards in their defensive pack.

The whole idea behind 'catenaccio' is that by employing the 'libero' or 'free back' behind the conventional stopper centre-half, the defence always has an extra man to call upon.

Now if by sheer speed off the mark in an unexpected burst I can leave my guardian full-back flat-footed, I have succeeded in levelling the odds. The 'libero' must come to meet the threat, and the other defenders no longer have that security of mind that if they are beaten, there is someone behind them to mop up.

Against the set pattern which the 'catenaccio' presents, unpredictability is perhaps the strongest weapon of all. I try never to repeat a move during a match and to always keep the opposition guessing.

Variations in pace, altering my line of approach and gaining that split-second advantage over the man marking me, are all part of this.

I have seen bigger, stronger wingers than myself stopped time after time because the man who is marking them has summed up their stereotyped moves.

As Soccer players go I am small, standing 5 foot 5 inches tall and weighing 10 stone 13 pounds. But

strangely enough this has been one of my biggest advantages.

Split-second shooting is invariably a question of balance and agility, and my compact physique is ideally adapted for this. Also, look at your own Jimmy Greaves and Alan Ball . . .

Nor am I alone in this, for two of the wingers who have been able to cause havoc with the 'catenaccio' – Chislenko of Russia and Johnstone of Celtic – are far from being in the 'weight-lifter' category!

Perhaps the greatest exponent of my 'mobility, speed and unpredictability' formula was England's own Sir Stanley Matthews. I am convinced that the most expert 'catenaccio' defence in existence wouldn't have been capable of holding him.

Whatever your views on this defensively minded Soccer it has to be admitted that it is effective in its purpose of preventing your opponents from scoring. Although it has been condemned in England perhaps more than in any other country, English clubs playing in two-leg European competitions have themselves adopted it.

There is, however, one criticism that has been aimed at it that I won't go along with: that its

'stop the opposition' attitude has led to excessively rough play.

During my long stay in Italy I have no complaints on that score. True there is a lot of shirt-tugging, pushing and obstruction.

But I maintain that Soccer is much safer here than in those countries where they get stuck in like gladiators. The fact that Soccer in Italy is brainy rather than brawny has helped me play for eleven years without collecting any scars.

There is method in Italian fouls . . . rarely malice. Tempers may flare up after the ball has been played, but there are very few 'scarponi', as they call them here – that is, men who deliberately put the boot in

That's why I reckon that I still have three or fou seasons of top-class Soccer left in me, or at leas enough time to score the 20 goals I need to take m over the 200 mark.

Tactics in football are changing all the time During my time I have seen the birth of th 'catenaccio' and its development into a dominatin, factor in the game.

In the last couple of years there is evidence tha it is being overtaken by new tactics. Who knows? may still be around to see its decline and fina disappearance.

A great save by George Niven, scraping the ball off Alan Anderson's feet in a Partick v. Hearts game . . .

THE FOOTBALL SWORD OF HONOUR 1968

GLASGOW OBSERVER

CELTIC MAKE HISTORY

The Editors and Publisher of the
International Football Book
announce the award of the
1968 Football Sword of Honour
to Mr. JOCK STEIN
Manager of Glasgow Celtic F.C.

Jock brought modern tactics to the Scots

by JOHN BLAIR
Scottish Sports Editor of " The People"

YOU'VE got to know Jock Stein really well to appreciate his football genius – and by 'know him' I don't mean the casual weekly meeting before or after a match, or the midweek visit to a training session. I mean know what he's thinking.

Although Jock was good, sometimes very good, in his four years as a Celtic player, he wasn't the Soccer magician he is now. He has become a better manager than he was a player. But he's a great manager for the same reason that he was a good player.

Jock 'thinks' football.

A match to him isn't simply a pitch, a ball and eleven a side. Not by a very long chalk. Indeed I don't know anyone who thinks more deeply about the game in general, and each game in particular.

Yet he's got a happy sense of humour. Like the Monday morning a photographer from a national daily called at Parkhead for a picture of a Celtic player. 'You shouldn't be here,' Jock nailed him 'you should be at Ibrox.'

Puzzled, wondering if perhaps his paper had telephoned changing his instructions, the photographer

Homecoming for a hero . . . and the placards talk of History.

The winner! Steve Chalmers (centre) touches home the famous second goal against Inter.–Milan in Lisbon . . . goalkeeper Giuliano Sarti is left standing while Celtic become the first British side to take the European Cup.

'*The greatest thing ever to happen to Jock*' – More excitement from that European Cup Final. ABOVE, *a marvellous goal-line save by Sarti from Chalmers;* BELOW, *Sarti again – a great stop against Jimmy Johnstone;* FACING PAGE, *veteran Ronnie Simpson pulls out a good 'un to beat the inrushing Giacinto Facchetti.*

repeated, but a little uncertainly, that he'd been told to go to Parkhead. Then Jock got in the punch line.

'I saw you behind the goal when I was watching Rangers on TV on Saturday night,' he said, 'and I saw you throw your arms up in the air when they scored the winner. That's why you should be at Ibrox. Not here.'

There were plenty of photographers and reporters on hand, of course, when Celtic won the European Champions' Cup. That was the greatest thing ever to happen to Jock and I'll never forget that day in Lisbon when Inter.-Milan had been beaten and it was all over bar the celebrations.

All the fears and worries were forgotten. Jock was as happy as a sand-boy in the luxurious Palacio Hotel in Estoril, outside the Portuguese capital. He 'threatened' to throw Tommy Gemmell into the

when they knocked Celtic out of the European Cu And when 'Celts' were knocked out of the Scotti Cup in the first round by Dunfermline, a resu which must have shaken Jock's Soccer world to i very foundations, he was able to say: 'Dunfermlir were the better team on the day. They deserve their victory. We wish them well in the competitior

But don't get the idea the Celtic boss is one of tl game's great losers. He isn't. No man who is ambitious for his club as Jock is for Celtic could l a good loser, of course. Jock lives for Celtic. Mal no mistake.

I have known him for close on twenty years and know he has two interests in life – his family ar football. And for football you can read Celtic! F set out to make them a great side, and he did it – Lisbon!

Much of his Soccer success, I'm sure, is due to tl

Shirtless, surrounded . . . but undeniably happy : it's Celtic captain Billy McNeill seconds after that European Cup Final win . . .

pool for ragging him; he entertained a stream of Celtic fans who poured in to offer their congratulations; he gave dozens of interviews to the top men of press, T.V. and radio from almost every European country.

In victory or defeat, Jock Stein has the quality of humility. In success, for example, he is always mindful of the beaten opposition – and in defeat, although he may feel shattered, he always tries to give honour where honour is due.

He was ready to pay tribute to Dynamo Kiev

support of his wife and family. Like most manage he never fully relaxes at home, but his wife Jea has the ability to help him share his successes ar defeats.

Many times I've called him on the telephone or to be told he was out kicking a ball with his sc George, or had gone down the road to see a bc who was sick – a boy, incidentally, who might we be a true-blue Rangers fan. It has happened mo than once.

Jock may be Celtic through and through, but I

as no time for bigotry. While he never hides his dedication to his own club, he can't stand people who see no good in the other team. 'If you're going to think about the game,' he says, 'you've got to watch both sides.' And Jock has always thought about football.

His ex-colleague Bertie Peacock, the former Northern Ireland international and team manager, once told me indeed: '*Jock was the man who introduced modern tactics to Scottish football.* Until he came to Parkhead there were no real plans before a game. But after he was appointed captain he made it known what he wanted done . . . and nobody resented this new trend because we all knew Jock was a player's man.'

He's still a player's man. I believe that was one of the reasons why Celtic won the European Cup. Jock is the first to admit his team may not have compared individually with some of the more illustrious European sides, but he had something many of the top European managers didn't have. *He had the respect and confidence of his players.*

He used to be amused, however, by the praise lavished on him, the talk about his magic formula for instant success. He operates in fact on a most uncomplicated principle.

'No manager can survive with bad players,' he says, 'so I try to turn them into good players, or at least to bring out the best in them. I remind them of the importance of listening and carrying out instructions, and of gaining confidence in themselves. There's nothing very magical in that.'

What's worth mentioning, however, even if it doesn't come into the category of magic, is that in my own fairly close connection with the Celtic players, and while I've heard them criticise the boss for something he made them do – an extra training stint perhaps, or for refusing to let them out on a foreign trip – I have never heard anyone accuse him of being unfair.

And that's something I know Jock Stein cares about, although you won't hear him boasting about it. But then you don't hear him boasting. He will tell you, however, about one of his great Soccer disappointments – Scotland's failure to qualify for the last World Cup finals.

I remember the day in Naples when, as Scotland team boss, he had to reorganise his line-up at the last minute. Rangers' Willie Henderson was a late call-off and, with no Law or Baxter in the side, the Scots were really up against it.

They lost to the Italians and were eliminated. Jock was as disappointed as I think I've ever seen him. He'd taken the Scotland job under severe pressure. His first loyalty, he had insisted, was to Celtic, but he'd promised to do everything he could for the national side – and he had certainly kept his word.

Defeat was a poor reward for the effort involved, but there was some slight consolation. Before he took over he was told: 'You'll never tame Law and Baxter – they're big heads.'

Jock's reply when the three-game stint was over was: 'I got all the respect from Law and Baxter a manager could ask. They were both first-class.'

If there's anything magical about the Stein success story as a manager – first with Dunfermline then with Hibs and now with Celtic – it's the respect players always seem to have for him. Why?

He's been named Britain's Manager of the Year two years in succession, and I clearly recall him saying on both occasions: '*The players won the award for me.*' That could be the reason!

For old-time Celtic fans, Willie Maley is synonymous with great Parkhead feats. But Jock Stein is the modern crusader, the man who did what no other British manager had done . . . brought the European Cup to this Soccer-daft island. A prestige boost for Britain of which Jock is rightly if quietly proud.

What does the future hold for him? In season 1966–67 he won for Celtic every major tourney in which they participated – something which can't be done every year, not even by a Jock Stein.

But I'm convinced he'll make Celtic a great European team again. That's the job to which he's dedicated . . . and for which he has shown he has the exceptional talent necessary.

Steve Chalmers again . . . heading in a sixth-minute goal which raced Celtic into the lead against Dundee.

Big Fees Hasten European League

'Why not a British Competition?'

by JOCK STEIN

(Manager of Glasgow Celtic)

FOR a country of its size Scotland can rightly be proud of its Soccer record. With little more than a five million population we can hold our heads high in world Soccer. Our record in the World Cup may not be outstanding, but we have been on the verge of really big success on more than one occasion.

I'm proud to say my own club Celtic, by winning the European Club Championship, probably gave Scotland its greatest competitive club honour of all time.

With a team composed entirely of home Scots, and not a

single fabulous-transfer star from any other country, we beat the best in Europe . . . to the surprise of many.

We did what no other British team has ever done and primarily, of course, it brought success and acclaim to Parkhead. But it also made many people in the world realise Scotland is *not* a decadent Soccer nation.

I know we were shock winners. I heard the rumblings before we faced Vojvodina (Yugoslavia), and Dukla (Prague), and then the fabulous Inter.-Milan from Italy in the Final. Comments like: *'Celtic will never do it – they're not in the same class.'*

It was suggested we were incapable of getting even to the quarter finals, never heed the Final. But we *did* get through to the Final; we *did* win . . . and in the humblest way I think we did it well. No matter what lies ahead, or what went before, Celtic won the European Champions' Cup for Scotland and for Britain.

Not even the cynics can scrub that feat from the record books.

Our success in Europe earned me, unworthily I think, the tag 'British Manager of the Year' for two years in succession. But I don't kid myself about this success, or any other which attended Celtic in

their great run. *Good players make good managers, and that's what I have at Parkhead.*

Without the full co-operation of my players there would have been no European success. I expected a lot from my players, and got it. In return I gave them all I had.

Sometimes when I reflect on that wonderful day in Lisbon, it all seems a dream. As I watch the film of the game – and I've watched it hundreds of times now – I get the queer feeling that Steve Chalmers' winning goal won't happen. But, thank goodness, it always does!

It's no new thought that we Scots are dour and determined, but no group of players were ever more determined to succeed than mine. That's the main reason Scotland and Celtic have made their mark in world football . . . and will continue to do so, no matter what the knockers say.

While I don't foresee a British Cup or British League for us to try to win in the near future, it's something I'd like to see happen, because to me it means progress. We at Parkhead have no fear of a British competition. We're satisfied we can hold our own with any team in the country, north or south of the border.

The know-alls who say Celtic, or Rangers, wouldn't last a season in a British League know nothing. In recent years, for example, we have beaten Manchester United, Sunderland and drawn with Spurs – and don't let anyone kid you these were 'just friendlies'. They were as tough and hard as any Cup-tie or League game.

I don't see any kind of British formation materialising, of course, until we get some kind of league reconstruction. There's got to be a trimming of the leagues in Scotland, and there's no use clubs saying: 'It's the rules.'

The clubs in membership of the Scottish League make the rules . . . so if they *want*, they can have them changed. There isn't a thing in the world to stop them, except perhaps a lack of courage and foresight which never fails to amaze me.

It never fails to amaze me, either, the number of people in football who really should know better but who look back on the past through rose-tinted 'specs'. There's hardly a week or a quiz-night passes without someone saying to me: 'The players of

Football's drama of the unexpected . . . it's Ranger's first goal against Celtic in their New Year's Day clash, a shot from Willie Johnston which trickled through 'keeper John Fallon's legs. And nobody, but nobody can believe it!

today are not nearly as good as they were twenty years ago.'

To me that's a load of old rubbish!

The players of today are as good as the players of the past. It's simply that the greybeards who think the game has gone back had a different approach twenty years ago. They were younger for one thing . . . and none of us lightly gives up the idols of his youth.

But if you really look for them, as managers have to do, you'll find players today who can compare with the past.

What may be lacking, I admit, are some of the outstanding personalities who used to adorn the Scottish game. But although personality may ha dimmed a little, the class of player hasn't.

Scotland is producing as many top-class playe today as ever before. Having said that, however, agree the transfer market has gone raving mad. I in this direction that the game – and not only Scotland – has lost its way. *The very idea of hundre thousand-pounds-plus transfers gives me the shivers.*

The game just can't stand deals like that especially if the prices are to go on rising as th are doing now. It can mean nothing but damag Irreparable damage. It makes the big clubs bigg and snuffs the small clubs out of existence.

The small clubs who unearth a good player a

Celtic in dominating mood (BELOW) . . . *Bobby Lennox hails the third of his four goals against Partick Thistle at Firhill.* FACING PAGE, *Celtic's Bobby Murdoch shows his power in this clearance from Dundee United's Rolland, who has every reason to look a bit apprehensive . . .*

reap the benefits of a big transfer may seem to be in clover, it's true. But only temporarily – for while they have a few bob in the bank, they don't have a team on the field. Certainly not a team to live against the big boys.

Nothing can lead to the formation of a European League quicker than this transfer escalation.

Make no mistake. Any club who pay out £125,000 for a player want it back, and they won't get it from the ordinary League fare. *Europe is the place to get it back . . .* and the small clubs won't be there!

Europe has its headaches, however, as I know. After our now infamous experiences in South America against Racing of Argentine, I am often asked: 'Would you consider going back?'

Strangely enough, the answer is 'Yes.' Hesitantly perhaps, but 'Yes'.

World football must progress and our unhappy experiences mustn't be allowed to close the door. If what happened to us can be the means of it n happening to some other British side on some futu occasion, then it will have been worthwhile.

Mind you, nothing will ever alter my feeling about what happened to my players in the thre games for the World Club Championship, but would be turning my back on the prospect progress if I were to say: 'Never again.'

Before the world-title games were played, don forget, F.I.F.A. couldn't have cared less. The didn't even send a representative. They labelle the games 'friendlies' – there was a misnomer you like – and refused a request from the S.F.A. t send a representative to the third and final gam

Their mood has now changed in the light of ou experience. All of a sudden the World Champion ship games have become important and F.I.F.A have decided to take a direct interest in future. *change of heart which is progress in itself.*

Looks like a goal for diving Willie Johnston of Rangers (in white shirt), but Falkirk's No. 3 Hunter cleared this header off the line.

SPOTLIGHT MAINLY ON EUROPE

THE most important international matches played during 1967 and the first quarter of 1968 were those affecting qualification for the quarter-finals of the European Football Championship – the re-styled European Nations Cup. The qualifying competition, in which 31 countries were allocated to eight groups with the group-winners qualifying for a place in the quarter-finals, was scheduled for completion by the end of 1967. In fact three matches spilled over into 1968, by which time Italy had made certain of qualification in Group VI and there was no group significance about Switzerland's visit to Nicosia to play against Cyprus. It was important to the Cypriots however, and Olympiakos of Nicosia had their league match in the Greek First Division (where they now play) postponed for the occasion. The Swiss sent their strongest available side with five 1966 World Cup players, and most of the remainder were younger players who had gained regular places in the national side since the summer of 1966. Cyprus gave Switzerland an early goal when Kostas put through his own goal but then the Cypriots scored twice (Melis and Lamboulis) without reply for a rare win over the 'A' side of a European association.

The two other 1968 E.F.C. qualifying matches concerned the British 'four' competing in Group VIII. Again one of these, between Wales and Northern Ireland, had no group significance, but the other, between Scotland and England, was all-important. Simply the position was that Scotland, the home country, had seven points from three wins, a draw and one defeat; England had eight points from four wins and one defeat. Scotland thus needed to win to qualify, England could be content with avoiding defeat – and did precisely that in drawing one-all. Important as this match was, the result that effectively determined the English qualification was Northern Ireland's one-nil win over Scotland the previous October. Throughout the qualifying competition there were examples of where the failure to qualify resulted from the loss of points against inferior opposition – or perhaps I should write *assumed* inferior position?

The failure of both West Germany (second placed in the 1966 World Championship) and Portugal (third placed) can be squarely attributed to this slackness. In the case of Portugal, it was in the opening match in the group competition (in November 1966) that they were beaten at home by Sweden. On the same day Bulgaria won their home match against Norway and ever after Portugal were travelling uphill. In the last two matches played in the group, Bulgaria won at home (1–0) and played a goalless match away, both against Portugal, to emphasise their entitlement to the group leadership – but it was Portugal's initial lapse at home that had so seriously jeopardised their chances. Thereafter they had to hope for a slip by Bulgaria – as England did in respect of Scotland. Bulgaria made no such slip: Scotland did.

The West German failure was more remarkable than that of Portugal because they travelled to Tirana to play Albania knowing exactly what was required – a simple victory. Not a lot to ask from the beaten World Cup finalists against the most isolated of all the world's footballing nations whose participation in international matches since 1958 has been limited to home and away matches against Denmark (in the last European Nations Cup), and against the Netherlands, Switzerland and Northern Ireland (in the 1966 World Cup qualifying competition). In 1963 Albania had gained a one-nil home win over Denmark and in 1965 they had drawn one-all against Northern Ireland, otherwise their record had been one of defeat – as it was against Yugoslavia home and away and West Germany away in the European Championship. But now, in December 1967, they played a goalless match against West Germany – and Yugoslavia had qualified for the European quarter-finals on West Germany's failure.

Spain owed their qualification for the quarter-finals to an even more remarkable failure on the part of a fancied rival, Czechoslovakia. Spain had seemed to have spoiled their own chances of retaining the European title (they were the winners, at home, of the last Nations Cup competition) when they drew their away matches against the Republic of Ireland and Turkey. The Czechs, on the other hand, collected both points in Dublin. Spain and Czechoslovakia each won their home match against each other, and when Spain had completed their programme of six matches they had gained eight points. Czechoslovakia had six points with two matches to play – against Turkey away and the Republic of Ireland at home. Spain had virtually accepted defeat – their players said goodbye to the bonus they had been promised if Spain reached the quarter-finals. Even when the match in Istanbul was goalless it seemed impossible that the Czechs, with better goal-average and goal-difference than Spain, would fail to at least draw at home against the Irish. But they lost by the odd goal in three!

There is ample warning in the results of the European Football Championship (set out overleaf) to all national team managers – in qualifying competitions there are no 'soft' matches!

GORDON JEFFERY

133

EUROPEAN FOOTBALL CHAMPIONSHIP
QUALIFYING COMPETITION

Group I

Rep. of Ireland	0	Spain	0
Rep. of Ireland	2	Turkey	1
Spain	2	Rep. of Ireland	0
Turkey	0	Spain	0
Turkey	2	Rep. of Ireland	1
Rep. of Ireland	0	Czechoslovakia	2
Spain	2	Turkey	0
Czechoslovakia	3	Turkey	0
Czechoslovakia	1	Spain	0
Spain	2	Czechoslovakia	1
Turkey	0	Czechoslovakia	0
Czechoslovakia	1	Rep. of Ireland	2

	P	W	D	L	Pts
Spain	6	3	2	1	8
Czechoslovakia	6	3	1	2	7
Rep. of Ireland	6	2	1	3	5
Turkey	6	1	2	3	4

Group II

Bulgaria	4	Norway	
Portugal	1	Sweden	
Sweden	ì	Portugal	
Norway	1	Portugal	
Sweden	0	Bulgaria	
Norway	0	Bulgaria	
Norway	3	Sweden	
Sweden	5	Norway	
Bulgaria	3	Sweden	
Portugal	2	Norway	
Bulgaria	1	Portugal	
Portugal	0	Bulgaria	

	P	W	D	L	Pts
Bulgaria	6	4	2	0	10
Portugal	6	2	2	2	6
Sweden	6	2	1	3	5
Norway	6	1	1	4	3

Group III

Finland	0	Austria	0
Greece	2	Finland	1
Finland	1	Greece	1
U.S.S.R.	4	Austria	3
U.S.S.R.	4	Greece	0
U.S.S.R.	2	Finland	0
Finland	2	U.S.S.R.	5
Austria	2	Finland	1
Greece	4	Austria	1
Austria	1	U.S.S.R.	0
Greece	0	U.S.S.R.	1
Austria	1	Greece	1

(abandoned after 85 mins.)

	P	W	D	L	Pts
U.S.S.R.	6	5	0	1	10
Greece	6	2	2	2	6
Austria	6	2	2	2	6
Finland	6	0	2	4	2

Group IV

W. Germany	6	Albania	
Yugoslavia	1	W. Germany	
Albania	0	Yugoslavia	
W. Germany	3	Yugoslavia	
Yugoslavia	4	Albania	
Albania	0	W. Germany	

	P	W	D	L	Pts
Yugoslavia	4	3	0	1	6
W. Germany	4	2	1	1	5
Albania	4	0	1	3	1

Group V

Netherlands	2	Hungary	2
Hungary	6	Denmark	0
Netherlands	2	Denmark	0
E. Germany	4	Netherlands	3
Hungary	2	Netherlands	1
Denmark	0	Hungary	2
Denmark	1	E. Germany	1
Netherlands	1	E. Germany	0
Hungary	3	E. Germany	1
Denmark	3	Netherlands	2
E. Germany	3	Denmark	2
E. Germany	1	Hungary	0

	P	W	D	L	Pts
Hungary	6	4	1	1	9
E. Germany	6	3	1	2	7
Netherlands	6	2	1	3	5
Denmark	6	1	1	4	3

Group VI

Rumania	4	Switzerland	
Italy	3	Rumania	
Cyprus	1	Rumania	
Cyprus	0	Italy	
Rumania	7	Cyprus	
Switzerland	7	Rumania	
Rumania	0	Italy	
Italy	5	Cyprus	
Switzerland	5	Cyprus	
Switzerland	2	Italy	
Italy	4	Switzerland	
Cyprus	2	Switzerland	

	P	W	D	L	Pts
Italy	6	5	0	1	11
Rumania	6	3	0	3	6
Switzerland	6	2	1	3	5
Cyprus	6	1	0	5	2

Group VII

Poland	4	Luxembourg	0
France	2	Poland	1
Belgium	2	France	1
Luxembourg	0	France	3
Luxembourg	0	Belgium	5
Luxembourg	0	Poland	0
Poland	3	Belgium	1
Poland	1	France	4
Belgium	2	Poland	4
France	1	Belgium	1
Belgium	3	Luxembourg	0
France	3	Luxembourg	1

	P	W	D	L	Pts
France	6	4	1	1	9
Belgium	6	3	1	2	7
Poland	6	3	1	2	7
Luxembourg	6	0	1	5	1

Group VIII

N. Ireland	0	England	
Wales	1	Scotland	
England	5	Wales	
Scotland	2	N. Ireland	
N. Ireland	0	Wales	
England	2	Scotland	
Wales	0	England	
N. Ireland	1	Scotland	
England	2	N. Ireland	
Scotland	3	Wales	
Scotland	1	England	
Wales	2	N. Ireland	

	P	W	D	L	Pts
England	6	4	1	1	9
Scotland	6	3	2	1	8
Wales	6	1	2	3	4
N. Ireland	6	1	1	4	3

ENGLAND

	A	B	C	D	E	F	G
Banks	G	—	—	G	G	G	G
Bonetti	—	G	G	—	—	—	—
Cohen	RB	RB	—	RB	RB	—	—
Newton	—	LB	RB	LB	—	—	RB
Knowles	—	—	—	—	—	RB	—
Wilson	LB	—	LB	—	LB	LB	LB
Stiles	RH	—	—	—	—	—	—
Mullery	—	RH	RH	RH	RH	RH	RH
J. Charlton	CH	—	—	CH	—	—	—
Labone	—	CH	CH	—	—	—	CH
Sadler	—	—	—	—	CH	CH	—
Moore	LH	LH	LH	LH	LH	LH	LH
Ball	OR	OR	OR	OR	—	OR	OR
Thompson	—	—	—	—	OR	—	—
Greaves	IR	IR	IR	—	—	—	—
Hunt	—	CF	CF	IR	IR	IR	—
Hurst	IL	IL	IL	IL	IL	IL	IR
R. Charlton	CF	—	—	CF	CF	CF	IL
Summerbee	—	—	—	—	—	—	CF
Peters	OL	—	—	OL	OL	OL	OL
Hollins	—	OL	—	—	—	—	—
Hunter	—	—	OL	—	—	—	—

ITALY

	A	B	C	D	E	F
Sarti	G	G	—	—	—	—
Albertosi	—	—	G	G	G	G
Burgnich	RB	—	—	RB	RB	RB
Narbin	—	RB	—	—	—	—
Gori	—	—	RB	—	—	—
Facchetti	LB	LB	LB	LB	LB	LB
Lodetti	RH	RH	—	—	—	—
Bertini	—	—	RH	—	—	—
Fogli	—	—	—	RH	—	—
Rosato	—	—	—	—	RH	—
Ferrini	—	—	—	—	—	RH
Guarneri	CH	CH	CH	—	—	—
Picchi	LH	LH	LH	CH	CH	CH
Bercellino	—	—	—	LH	LH	LH
Domenghini	OR	IR[2]	—	OR	OR	OR
Bulgarelli	—	OR	IL	—	—	—
Rivera	IR	IR[1]	OR	—	—	IL
Juliano	IL	—	IR	IR	IR	IR
Cappellini	CF	IL	—	—	—	—
Mazzola	—	CF	—	CF	—	CF
Zigoni	—	—	CF	—	—	—
Boninsegna	—	—	—	—	CF	—
Riva	—	IL	—	OL	OL	OL
Corso	OL	OL	—	—	—	—
Pascutti	—	—	OL	—	—	—
De Sisti	—	—	—	IL	IL	—

HUNGARY

A	22. 4. 67	Hungary 1 (Bene)	Yugoslavia 0	—	Budapest
B	10. 5. 67	Hungary 2 (Meszoly, Farkas)	Netherlands 1 (Suurbier)	—	Budapest
C	24. 5. 67	Denmark 0	Hungary 2 (Sandvad o.g., Albert)	—	Copenhagen
D	6. 9. 67	Austria 1 (Hof)	Hungary 3 (Bene, Farkas, Varga)	—	Vienna
E	27. 9. 67	Hungary 3 (Farkas 3)	E. Germany 1 (Frenzel)	—	Budapest
F	29. 10. 67	E. Germany 1 (Frenzel)	Hungary 0	—	Leipzig
G	6. 12. 67	Mexico 2 (Borja, Bustos)	Hungary 1 (Varga)	—	Mexico City
H	9. 12. 67	Mexico 0	Hungary 2 (Dunai, Bene)	—	Guadalajara
I	13. 12. 67	Chile 4	Hungary 5 (Farkas 3, Bene, Molnar)	—	Santiago

	A	B	C	D	E	F	G	H	I
Tamasz	G	G	G	G	G	G	G[1]	—	G[2]
Gelei	—	—	—	—	—	—	G[2]	G	G[1]
Kaposzta	RB	—	—	RB	RB	RB	RB	RB	RB
Matrai	—	RB	RB	RH	RH	—	—	—	—
Meszoly	RH	RH	RH	—	—	—	—	—	—
Ihasz	LB	LB	LB	LB	LB	LB	—	—	—
Sovari	—	—	—	—	—	—	LB	LB	LB
Pancsis	—	—	—	—	—	RH	RH	RH	RH
Szucs	CH	CH	CH	CH	CH	CH	CH	CH	CH
Rakosi	LH	LH	LH	LH	LH	LH	LH[1]	—	OL[2]
Molnar	OR	OR	OR	—	—	—	—	—	CF[2]
Bene	CF	CF	CF	OR	OR	OR	OR	OR	OR
Varga	IR	—	—	IR	IR	IR	IR[1]	IR	IR
Gorocs	—	IR	—	IL[2]	IL	—	IL	IL	IL
I. Nagy	—	—	IR	—	—	—	—	—	—
Albert	IL	IL	IL	CF	CF	CF	—	—	—
Dunai	—	—	—	—	—	—	CF	CF	CF[1]
Zambo	—	—	—	—	—	—	IR[2]	—	—
Mathesz	—	—	—	IL[1]	—	IL	LH[2]	LH	LH
Farkas	OL	OL	OL	OL	OL	OL	OL	OL	OL[1]

SOVIET UNION

A	10. 5. 67	Scotland	0	U.S.S.R.	2	—	Glasgow
				(Gemmell o.g., Medvid)			
B	28. 5. 67	U.S.S.R. (Chislenko, Bishovets)	2	Mexico	0	—	Leningrad
C	3. 6. 67	France (Gondet, Simon)	2	U.S.S.R. (Chislenko 2, Bishovets, Streltzov)	4	—	Paris
D	11. 6. 67	U.S.S.R. (Malafeyev, Bishovets, Chislenko, Streltzov)	4	Austria (Hof, Wolny, Sieber)	3	—	Moscow
E	16. 7. 67	U.S.S.R. (Banichevski 2, Sabo, Chislenko)	4	Greece	0	—	Tbilisi
F	28. 7. 67	Poland	0	U.S.S.R. (Chislenko)	1	—	Wroclaw
G	4. 8. 67	U.S.S.R. (Chislenko, Banichevski)	2	Poland (Lubanski)	1	—	Moscow
H	30. 8. 67	U.S.S.R. (Khurtsilava, Chislenko)	2	Finland	0	—	Moscow
I	6. 9. 67	Finland (Peltonen, Syrjavaara)	2	U.S.S.R. (Sabo 2, Chislenko, Banichevski, Malafeyev)	5	—	Turku
J	1. 10. 67	U.S.S.R. (Khurtsilava, Pfirter o.g.)	2	Switzerland (Blattler, Perroud)	2	—	Moscow
K	8. 10. 67	Bulgaria (Dermendiev)	1	U.S.S.R. (Streltzov, Banichevski)	2	—	Sofia
L	15. 10. 67	Austria (Grausam)	1	U.S.S.R.	0	—	Vienna
M	31. 10. 67	Greece	0	U.S.S.R. (Malafeyev)	1	—	Athens
N	29. 11. 67	Netherlands (Wery 2, Romeijn)	3	U.S.S.R. (Khurtsilava)	1	—	Rotterdam
O	6. 12. 67	England (Ball, Peters)	2	U.S.S.R. (Chislenko 2)	2	—	Wembley
P	16. 12. 67	Chile (Reynoso)	1	U.S.S.R. (Moris o.g., Streltzov 3)	4	—	Santiago

	A	B	C	D	E	F	G	H	I	J	K	L	M	N	O	P
Yashin	G	G	G¹	G	G	—	—	—	—	—	—	—	—	—	—	—
Kavazashvili	—	—	G²	—	—	—	—	G	—	—	G	G	G	—	—	—
Psenitchnikov	—	—	—	—	—	G	G	—	G	G	—	—	—	G	G	G
Afonin	RB	LH	LB	RB	—	RB	RB	RB	RB	RB	—	RB	RB	RB	—	—
Lenev	—	RB	RB	LB	RB	—	—	—	—	—	—	—	—	—	—	—
Czechovrebov	—	—	—	—	—	LB	LB	LB	—	LB	RB	LB	LB	RH	—	—
Istomin	—	—	—	—	—	—	—	—	—	—	—	—	—	LB	RB	RB
Danilov	LB	LB	—	—	—	—	—	—	—	—	—	—	—	—	—	—
Anichkine	—	—	—	—	LB	—	—	—	CH	LH	LB	RH	—	LH	LB	LB
Logofet	—	—	—	—	—	—	—	—	LB	—	—	—	—	—	—	—
Voronin	RH	RH	RH	—	RH	RH	RH	RH	—	—	—	—	RH	—	RH	RH
Maslov	—	—	—	—	—	—	—	—	RH	RH	—	RH	IR	—	IR	—
Morozov	—	—	—	—	—	—	—	—	—	RH	—	—	—	—	—	—
Chesternev	CH	CH	CH	—	CH	CH	CH	CH	—	CH	CH	CH	CH	CH	CH	CH
Khurtsilava	LH	—	—	LH	LH	LH	LH	LH	LH	LH	LH	LH	IL	LH	LH	LH
Sosnikhin	—	—	LH	—	—	—	—	—	—	—	—	—	—	—	—	—
Chislenko	OR	OR	OR¹	OR	OR	OR	OR	OR	OR	—	—	—	OR	OR	OR	OR
Jeskov	—	—	—	—	—	—	—	—	—	OR	—	—	—	—	—	—
Medved	IR	IR	IR	—	—	—	—	—	—	—	—	—	—	—	—	—
Banichevski	—	—	—	—	IR	IR	IR	CF	CF	CF	OR	OR	IR	CF	IR	IR¹
Streltzov	CF	CF	CF	IR	CF	CF	CF	—	—	—	CF	CF	CF	—	CF	CF
Sabo	IL	IL	IL	IL	IL	IL	IL	IL	IL	—	IL	IL	IL	—	IL	IL
Malafeyev	OL	—	—	OL	—	OL²	OL	IR	IR	IR	IR	—	OL	—	OL	OL
Bishovets	—	OL	OL¹	CF	OL	OL¹	—	OL	OL	—	—	OL	—	—	—	IR²
Evrnjikhin	—	—	OR²	—	—	—	—	—	OL¹	—	—	—	—	—	—	—
Kemniski	—	—	OL²	—	—	—	—	—	—	—	—	—	—	—	—	—
Tujaev	—	—	—	—	—	—	—	—	—	OL²	OL	—	—	—	—	—
Naodija	—	—	—	—	—	—	—	—	—	—	—	—	—	OL	—	—

SPAIN

A 1. 2. 67 Turkey .... 0 Spain .... 0 — Istanbul
B 24. 5. 67 England .... 2 Spain .... 0 — Wembley
         (Greaves, Hunt)
C 31. 5. 67 Spain .... 2 Turkey .... 0 — Bilbao
         (Grosso, Gento)
D 1. 10. 67 Czechoslovakia .... 1 Spain .... 0 — Prague
         (Horvath)
E 22. 10. 67 Spain .... 2 Czechoslovakia .... 1 — Madrid
         (Pirri, Garate) (Kuna)

	A	B	C	D	E
Iribar	G	G	G	G	G
Sanchis	RB	RB	RB	RB	—
Osoria	—	—	—	—	RB
Reija	LB	LB	LB	LB	LB
Pirri	RH	RH	—	RH	RH
Paquito	IR	—	RH	—	—
Gallego	CH	CH	CH	CH	CH
Glaria	—	IR	LH	—	—
Violeta	LH	LH	—	—	—
Tonono	—	—	—	LH	LH
Amancio	OR	OR	—	OR	OR

	A	B	C	D	E
Ufarte	—	—	OR	—	—
Adelardo	—	—	IR	IR	—
Marcial	—	—	—	—	IR
Grosso	CF	CF	CF	CF	—
Luis	—	—	—	—	CF
Velasquez	IL	—	—	—	—
Jose Maria	OL	IL	IL	OL	OL
Marcelino	—	—	—	IL	—
Garate	—	—	—	—	IL
Gento	—	OL	OL	—	—

FRANCE

A 22. 3. 67 France.................... 1 Rumania.................. 2 — Paris
         (Dogliani) (Fratila, Dridea)
B 3. 6. 67 France.................... 2 U.S.S.R. .... 4 — Paris
         (Gondet, Simon) (Chislenko 2, Bishovets, Streltzov)
C 17. 9. 67 Poland.................... 1 France .... 4 — Warsaw
         (Brychczy) (Herbin, Guy, Di Nallo 2)
D 27. 9. 67 W. Germany .... 5 France.................... 1 — West Berlin
         (Libuda, Muller, Siemensmeyer 2, Overath) (Bosquier)
E 28. 10. 67 France.................... 1 Belgium .... 1 — Nantes
         (Herbin) (Claessen)
F 23. 12. 67 France.................... 3 Luxembourg .... 1 — Paris
         (Loubet 3) (Klein)

	A	B	C	D	E	F
Eon	G[1]	G	—	—	—	—
Carnus	G[2]	—	—	—	—	—
Aubour	—	—	G	G	G	G
Lavaud	RB	—	—	—	—	—
de Michele	—	RB	—	—	—	—
Djorkaeff	—	—	RB	RB	RB	RB
Cardiet	LB	LB	—	—	—	—
Baeza	—	—	LB	LB	LB	LB
Provelli	RH[1]	—	—	—	—	—
Budzinski	RH[2]	—	—	—	—	—
Le Chenadec	—	RH	—	—	—	—
Mitoraj	—	—	RH	—	—	—
Quittet	—	—	—	RH	RH	RH
Piumi	CH	CH	—	—	—	—
Bosquier	—	—	CH	CH	CH	CH
Suaudeau	LH[1]	—	—	—	—	—
Bonnel	LH[2]	CF[2]	—	—	—	—
Deloffre	—	LH	—	—	—	—

	A	B	C	D	E	F
Herbin	—	—	LH	—	LH	—
Peri	—	—	—	LH	—	—
Krawczyk	—	—	—	—	—	LH
Blanchet	OR	OR	—	—	—	—
Herbet	—	—	OR	—	IR	—
Lech	IR	—	—	—	—	—
Guy	—	IR	IR	—	—	—
Gress	—	—	—	—	IR	—
Couecou	—	—	—	—	—	IR
Gondet	CF	CF[1]	—	OR	—	—
Di Nallo	—	—	CF	CF	OR	—
Revelli	—	—	—	—	CF	—
Szepaniak	—	—	—	—	—	CF
Dogliani	IL	—	—	—	—	—
Simon	—	IL	—	IL	—	—
Michel	—	—	IL	—	IL	IL
Loubet	OL	OL	OL	OL	OL	OR
Beretta	—	—	—	—	—	OL

YUGOSLAVIA

A	22. 4. 67	Hungary (Bene)	1	Yugoslavia	0	—	Budapest
B	3. 5. 67	Yugoslavia (Skoblar)	1	W. Germany	0	—	Belgrade
C	14. 5. 67	Albania	0	Yugoslavia (Zambata 2)	2	—	Tirana
D	7. 10. 67	W. Germany (Lohr, Muller, Seeler)	3	Yugoslavia (Zambata)	1	—	Hamburg
E	1. 11. 67	Netherlands (Swart)	1	Yugoslavia (Belin, Osim)	2	—	Rotterdam
F	12. 11. 67	Yugoslavia (Spreco, Osim 2, Lazarevic)	4	Albania	0	—	Belgrade

	A	B	C	D	E	F
Pantelic	G	G	—	G	—	—
Knezevic	—	—	G	—	—	—
Vukcevic	—	—	—	—	G	G
Fazlagic	RB	RB	RB	RB	RB	RB
Brnzic	LB	RH	LB	LB	—	—
Jusufi	—	LB	—	—	—	—
Ramljak	—	—	—	—	LB	—
Djordjevic	—	—	—	—	—	LB
Damjanovic	RH	—	—	—	CH	CH
Becejac	OR	IR	RH	IR	—	—
Nesticki	—	—	—	—	RH	—
Rasovic	CH	CH	CH	CH	—	—
Musovic	—	—	—	—	RH	—
Paunovic	—	—	—	—	—	RH

	A	B	C	D	E	F
Holcer	LH	LH	LH	LH	LH	LH
Melic	IL	OR	IL	—	—	—
Nadoveza	—	—	OR	—	—	—
Zambata	—	—	IR	OR	—	—
Lazarevic	—	—	—	—	OR	IR
Djajic	OL	OL	OL	OL	—	OR
Hasanagic	IR	CF	—	—	—	—
Belin	—	—	—	—	IR	—
Lamza	CF	—	CF	—	—	—
Skoblar	—	IL	—	CF	—	—
Spreco	—	—	—	—	CF	CF
Osim	—	—	—	IL	IL	IL
Rora	—	—	—	—	OL	OL

BULGARIA

A	22. 3. 67	W. Germany (Heynckes)	1	Bulgaria	0	—	Hanover
B	11. 6. 67	Sweden	0	Bulgaria (Jekov, Dermendiev)	2	—	Stockholm
C	29. 6. 67	Norway	0	Bulgaria	0	—	Oslo
D	8. 10. 67	Bulgaria (Dermendiev)	1	U.S.S.R. (Streltsov, Banichevski)	2	—	Moscow
E	12. 11. 67	Bulgaria (Kotkov, Mitkov, Asparouchov)	3	Sweden	0	—	Sofia
F	26. 11. 67	Bulgaria (Dermendiev)	1	Portugal	0	—	Sofia
G	17. 12. 67	Portugal	0	Bulgaria	0	—	Lisbon

	A	B	C	D	E	F	G
Simeonov	G	G	G	—	G	G	G
Bontchev	—	—	—	G	—	—	—
Chalamanov	RB	RB	RB	—	RB	RB	—
Gaidarski	—	—	—	RB	—	—	RB
Gaganelov	LB	LB	LB	LB	LB	LB	LB
Penev	RH	RH	RH	RH	RH	RH	RH
Dimitrov I	CH	CH	CH	CH	—	—	CH
Jetchev	LH	LH	LH	LH	CH	CH	LH
Kolev	—	—	—	—	LH	—	—
Davidov	—	—	—	—	—	LH	—

	A	B	C	D	E	F	G
Tsanev	OR	—	—	—	—	—	—
Popov	—	OR	—	OR	—	—	CF
Mitkov	—	—	OR	—	OL	OL	—
Bonev	IR	IR	IR	IR	IR	IR	IR
Asparouchov	CF	—	—	—	CF	CF	—
Jekov	—	CF	CF	CF	—	—	—
Yakimov	IL	IL	IL	IL	—	—	IL
Kotkov	—	—	—	—	IL	IL	OL
Dermendiev	OL	OL	OL	OL	OR	OR	OR

BRAZIL

A	25. 6. 67	Uruguay	0	Brazil	0	— Montevideo
B	28. 6. 67	Uruguay (Rocha 2)	2	Brazil (Paulo Borges 2)	2	— Montevideo
C	1. 7. 67	Uruguay (Rocha)	1	Brazil (Dirceu Lopez)	1	— Montevideo

	A	B	C		A	B	C
Felix	G	G	G	Piazza	IR	IR	IR
Jurandir	RB	RB	RB	Alcindo	CF	—	—
Sadi	LB	LB	LB	Edu	—	CF[1]	—
Everaldo	RH	RH	RH	Natal	—	CF[2]	OR
Dias	CH	CH	CH	Tostao	IL	IL	IL
Dirceu Lopez	LH	LH	LH	Volmir	OL	—	—
Paulo Borges	OR	OR	CF	Hilton	—	OL	OL

MEXICO

A	5. 1. 67	Mexico (Pereda, Borja 2)	3	Switzerland	0	— Mexico City
B	8. 1. 67	Mexico	0	Switzerland (Hosp, Blattler)	2	— Guadalajara
C	28. 5. 67	U.S.S.R. (Chislenko, Bishovets)	2	Mexico	0	— Leningrad
D	6. 12. 67	Mexico (Borja, Bustos)	2	Hungary (Varga)	1	— Mexico City
E	9. 12. 67	Mexico	0	Hungary (Dunai, Bene)	2	— Guadalajara

	A	B	C	D	E
Calderon	G	—	G	G	G
Vargas	—	G	—	—	—
Chaires	RB	RB	—	—	—
Alejandres	—	—	—	RB	RB
Jaureggui	LB	LB	LB	—	—
Mario Perez	—	—	—	LB[2]	LH
Del Aguila	RH	—	IL	—	—
Isidoro Diaz	—	RH[1]	RH	IL[1]	RH
Pullido	—	RH[2]	—	—	—
Regueiro	—	—	—	RH	IL
Del Muro	CH	—	LH	LH	—
Pena	—	CH	CH	CH	CH
Nunez	LH	—	—	IL[2]	LB
Guillermo Hernandez	OL[2]	LH	RB	LB[1]	—
Jorge Gomez	OR	—	OR	—	—
Bustos	—	OR[1]	—	OR[1]	—
Delgado	—	OR[2]	—	—	—
Morales	—	—	—	OR[2]	—
Albino	—	—	—	—	OR
Borja	IR	—	CF	IR	IR
Pereda	CF	IR	OL	—	—
Fragoso	—	—	IR	CF	CF
Valdivia	—	CF	—	—	—
Mendoza	IL	—	—	—	—
Munguia	—	IL[1]	—	—	—
Anaya	—	IL[2]	—	—	—
Padilla	OL[1]	—	OL[1]	—	—
Jara	—	OL	—	—	OL
Manolete Hernandez	—	—	OL[2]	—	—

WEST GERMANY

A	22. 2. 67	W. Germany	5	Morocco	1	—	Karlsruhe
		(Ulsass 2, Löhr, Zaczyk, Heynckes)		(Bouassa)			
B	22. 3. 67	W. Germany	1	Bulgaria	0	—	Hanover
		(Heynckes)					
C	8. 4. 67	W. Germany	6	Albania	0	—	Dortmund
		(Muller 4, Löhr 2)					
D	3. 5. 67	Yugoslavia	1	W. Germany	0	—	Belgrade
		(Skoblar)					
E	27. 9. 67	W. Germany	5	France	1	—	West Berlin
		(Libuda, Overath, Siemensmeyer 2, Muller)		(Bosquier)			
F	7. 10. 67	W. Germany	3	Yugoslavia	1	—	Hamburg
		(Löhr, Muller, Seeler)		(Zambata)			
G	22. 11. 67	Rumania	1	W. Germany	0	—	Bucharest
		(Ghergheli)					
H	17. 12. 67	Albania	0	W. Germany	0	—	Tirana
I	6. 3. 68	Belgium	1	W. Germany	3	—	Brussels

	A	B	C	D	E	F	G	H	I
Wolter	G	—	—	—	—	G	G	—	—
Maier	—	G	—	G	G	—	—	G	G
Tilkowski	—	—	G	—	—	—	—	—	—
Patzke	RB	RB	RB	RB	RB	RB	RB	RB	—
Vogts	—	—	—	LB	—	—	LB	—	RB
Hottges	LB	LB	LB	—	LB	LB	—	LB	LB
Beckenbauer	RH	—	RH	RH	RH[1]	—	RH	—	RH
Kramer	—	RH	—	—	—	—	—	—	—
Roth	—	—	—	—	RH	—	—	—	—
Netzer	—	—	—	—	—	—	—	RH	IR
Schulz	CH	CH	CH	CH	CH	CH	CH	CH	CH
Fichtel	LH	—	—	LH	—	—	—	—	LH
Weber	—	LH	LH	—	LH	LH	LH	LH	—
Herrmann	OR	OR	—	—	—	—	—	—	—
Dorfel	—	—	OR	—	—	—	—	—	—
Held	OL	—	—	OR	—	—	OR	—	—
Libuda	—	—	—	OR	—	OR	—	—	—
Siemensmeyer	—	—	—	—	IR	OR	IR	—	—
Laumen	—	—	—	—	—	—	—	—	OR
Ulsass	IR[1]	IR	IR	—	—	—	—	—	—
Zaczyk	IR[2]	—	—	—	—	—	—	—	—
Muller	—	—	CF	IR	RH[2]	IR	—	—	—
Kuppers	—	—	—	CF	—	—	IR	—	—
Heynckes	CF	CF	—	—	—	—	—	—	—
Seeler	—	—	—	—	CF	CF	CF	—	—
Meyer	—	—	—	—	—	—	—	CF	—
Löhr	IL[2]	OL	OL	OL	OL	OL	OL	OL	CF
Overath	IL[1]	IL	IL	IL	IL	IL	IL	IL	—
Koppel	—	—	—	—	—	—	—	—	IL
Volkert	—	—	—	—	—	—	—	—	OL

EAST GERMANY

A	5. 4. 67	E. Germany .... 4 (Vogel, Frenzel 3)	Netherlands .... 3 (Mulder, Keizer 2)	—	Leipzig
B	17. 5. 67	Sweden 0	E. Germany .... 1 (Noldner)	—	Halsingborg
C	4. 6. 67	Denmark................. 1 (Bjerre)	E. Germany .... 1 (Lowe)	—	Copenhagen
D	13. 9. 67	Netherlands .... 1 (Cruijff)	E. Germany 0	—	Amsterdam
E	27. 9. 67	Hungary .... 3 (Farkas 3)	E. Germany .... 1 (Frenzel)	—	Budapest
F	11. 10. 67	E. Germany .... 3 (Korner, Pankau 2)	Denmark................. 2 (Dyreborg, Sondergaard)	—	Leipzig
G	29. 10. 67	E. Germany .... 1 (Frenzel)	Hungary 0	—	Leipzig
H	18. 11. 67	E. Germany .... 1 (Pankau)	Rumania................. 0	—	East Berlin
I	6. 12. 67	Rumania................. 0	E. Germany .... 1 (Irmscher)	—	Bucharest

	A	B	C	D	E	F	G	H	I
Weigang	G	—	—	—	—	—	—	—	—
Croy	—	G	G	—	G	—	—	—	—
Blochwitz	—	—	—	G	—	G	G	G	G
Fraesdorf	RB	RB	RB	RB	RB	—	—	—	—
Urbanczyk	—	—	—	—	—	RB	RB	RB	RB
Geisler	LB	LB	LB	LB	—	—	—	—	—
Bransch	—	LH	LH	LH	LB	LB	LB	LB	LB
Pankau	RH	—	—	RH	RH	RH	RH	RH	RH
Irmscher	—	RH	RH	IR	—	—	LH	IL	IL
Walter	CH	CH	CH	—	CH	CH	—	—	—
Wruck	—	—	—	CH	—	—	CH	CH	CH
Koerner	LH	IL	IL	—	LH	LH	—	—	—
Rock	—	—	—	—	—	—	—	LH	LH
R. Ducke	OR	OR	OR	OR	OR	OR	—	—	—
Hoge	—	—	—	—	—	—	OR	OR	OR
Noldner	IR	IR	IR	—	—	IR	IR	—	—
Frenzel	CF	CF	CF	CF	CF	CF	CF	CF	CF
Erler	IL	—	—	IL	IL	—	IL	IR	IR
P. Ducke	—	—	—	—	IR	IL	—	—	—
Vogel	OL	—	—	OL	OL	OL	—	OL	OL
Lowe	—	OL	OL	—	—	—	OL	—	—

RUMANIA

A	4. 1. 67	Uruguay .... 1 (Urrusmendi)	Rumania................. 1 (Varela o.g.)	—	Montevideo
B	8. 3. 67	Greece.................. 1 (Sideris)	Rumania................. 2 (Ionescu 2)	—	Athens
C	22. 3. 67	France.................. 1 (Dogliani)	Rumania................. 2 (Fratila, Dridea)	—	Paris
D	23. 4. 67	Rumania................. 7 (Lucescu, Martinovici, Dimitriu 3, Ionescu 2)	Cyprus 0	—	Bucharest
E	24. 5. 67	Switzerland .... 7 (Kunzli 2, Quentin 2, Blattler 2, Odermatt)	Rumania................. 1 (Dobrin)	—	Zurich

F	25. 6. 67	Rumania	0	Italy	1	—	Bucharest		

F   25. 6. 67   Rumania 0   Italy 1   —   Bucharest
                                                  (Bertini)
G   29. 10. 67 Poland 0   Rumania 0   —   Krakow
H   18. 11. 67 E. Germany 1   Rumania 0   —   East Berlin
                                                  (Pankau)
I   22. 11. 67 Rumania 1   W. Germany 0   —   Bucharest
                                                  (Ghergheli)
J   6. 12. 67   Rumania 0   E. Germany 1   —   Bucharest
                                                  (Irmscher)

	A	B	C	D	E	F	G	H	I	J
Constantinescu	G	G	—	—	—	—	—	—	—	—
M. Ionescu	—	—	G	G	G^1	—	—	—	—	—
Datcu	—	—	—	—	G^2	—	—	—	—	—
Raducanu	—	—	—	—	—	G	—	—	—	—
Coman	—	—	—	—	—	—	G	G	—	G
Haidu	—	—	—	—	—	—	—	—	G	—
Samareanu	RB	RB	RB^1	—	—	—	RB	RB	RB	RB
Popa	—	—	RB^2	RB	RB	—	—	—	—	—
Lupescu	—	—	—	—	—	RB	—	—	—	—
Deleanu	LB	—	—	—	—	—	—	—	—	—
Mocanu	—	LB	LB	LB	LB	LB	LB	LB	LB	LB
Naftanaila	RH	IL^2	—	—	—	IL	—	—	—	—
Ghergheli	—	RH	RH	RH	RH	RH	—	IR	RH	RH
Koszka	—	—	—	—	—	—	RH	RH	IR	IL
Boc	CH	—	—	—	—	—	—	—	—	—
Nunweiler III	—	CH	CH	CH	CH	CH	—	CH	CH	CH
Nicolae	—	—	—	LH	LH	—	CH	CH	CH	CH
Florea	LH	—	—	—	—	—	—	—	—	—
Dan Coe	—	LH	—	—	—	—	LH	LH	LH	LH
Dobrin	—	IL^1	LH	IL	IL	—	IL^2	IL	IL^1	—
Barbu	—	—	—	—	—	LH	—	—	—	—
Nasturescu	OR	—	—	—	—	—	OR	OR^1	—	—
Pircalab	—	OR	—	—	OR	—	—	—	OR	OR
Lucescu	—	OL^1	OR	OL	OL	OR	—	OR^2	—	—
Martinovici	—	—	—	OR	—	—	—	—	—	—
Fratila	IR	IR	IR	—	—	—	—	—	—	—
Dimitriu	OL^3	—	IL	IR	—	IR	—	—	—	—
Dridea	—	—	CF	—	IR	—	—	—	—	—
Constantin	—	—	—	—	—	—	IR	CF	IL^2	IR
J. Ionescu	CF	CF	—	CF	CF	CF	—	OL	CF	CF
Soo	—	—	—	—	—	CF	—	—	—	—
Libardi	IL	—	—	—	—	IL^1	—	—	—	—
Gyorfi	OL^1	—	—	—	—	—	—	—	—	—
Moldoveanu	OL^2	—	—	—	—	—	—	—	—	—
Radu	—	OL^2	—	—	—	—	—	—	—	—
Sorin Avram	—	—	OL	—	—	—	—	—	—	—
Nunweiler VI	—	—	—	—	OL	—	—	—	—	—
Kallo	—	—	—	—	—	—	OL^2	—	OL	OL^1
Voinea	—	—	—	—	—	—	OL^1	—	—	—
Sasu	—	—	—	—	—	—	—	—	—	OL^2

POLAND

	A	B	C	D	E	F	G
Kornek	G	G	G	—	—	—	—
Brol	—	—	—	G	—	—	—
Kostka	—	—	—	—	G	G	G
Strzalkowski	RB	CH	—	—	—	—	—
Kowalski	—	RB	RB	RB	RB	—	—
Piechniczek	—	—	—	—	—	RB	RB
Gmoch	LB	LB	LB	LB	LB	LB	LB
Anczok	RH	RH	RH	RH	RH	—	—
Brejza	—	—	—	—	—	RH	—
Szefer	—	—	—	—	—	LH	RH
Oslizlo	CH	—	CH	CH	CH	CH	CH
Szmidt	LH	LH	LH	LH	—	IL	LH[1]
Suski	—	IL	IL	IL	LH	—	—
Hausner	OR	—	—	—	—	—	—

	A	B	C	D	E	F	G
Sadek	—	OR	—	—	—	—	—
Gadocha	—	—	OR[1]	OL	OL	—	—
Jarosik	OL	—	OR[2]	—	—	—	IL[1]
Domarski	—	—	—	OR	—	—	—
Faber	—	—	—	—	OR	OL	OL
Zmijewski	—	—	—	—	—	OR	OR
Musialek	IR	—	—	—	—	—	—
Szoltysik	IL	IR	IR	IR	IL	—	—
Brychczy	—	—	—	—	IR	IR	IR
Lubanski	CF	CF	CF	CF	CF	CF	CF
Nieroba	—	—	—	—	—	—	IL[2]
Gomoluch	—	—	—	—	—	—	LH[2]
Liberda	—	OL	OL	—	—	—	—

AUSTRIA

(Match abandoned after 85 mins.)

	A	B	C	D	E	F	G
Pichler	G	G	—	—	—	—	—
Hodschar	—	—	G	—	—	—	—
Fuchsbichler	—	—	—	G	G	—	—
Harreither	—	—	—	—	—	G	G
Wartusch	RB	RB	—	—	—	—	—
Gebhardt	—	—	RB	RB	RB	RB	RB
Fak	LB	LB	LB	—	—	—	—
Fröhlich	—	—	—	LB	LB	LB	LB
Eschmuller	RH	RH	—	—	—	—	—
Eigenstiller	—	—	RH	RH	RH	RH	RH
Glechner	CH	CH	CH[1]	CH	CH	CH	CH
Ullmann	—	—	CH[2]	—	—	—	—
Sturmberger	LH	LH	—	LH	—	IL	—
Hof	—	IL	LH	—	—	—	—
Frank	—	—	—	—	—	LH	—

	A	B	C	D	E	F	G
Stamm	—	—	—	—	—	LH	LH
Köglberger	OR	—	—	—	—	—	—
Flögel	—	—	OR	IL	IL	IL	IR	—
Wolny	IR	IR	OR	IR	—	—	—
Mzetzler	—	—	—	OR	—	—	—
Fritsch	—	—	OL[2]	—	OR	—	—
Koleznik	—	—	—	—	—	OR	OR
Hasil	—	—	IR	—	—	—	—
Sieber	CF	CF	CF	—	IR	OL	IR
Grausam	—	—	—	CF	CF	CF	CF
Schmidt	IL	—	—	—	—	—	—
Skocik	—	—	—	—	—	—	IL
Parits	OL	—	—	—	—	—	—
Hörmayr	—	OL	—	—	—	—	—
Redl	—	—	OL[1]	OL	OL	—	OL